Development Co-operation Review Series

Ireland

1999 No. 35

Development Assistance Committee

ORGANISATION FOR ECONOMIC CO-OPERATION AND DEVELOPMENT

ORGANISATION FOR ECONOMIC CO-OPERATION AND DEVELOPMENT

Pursuant to Article 1 of the Convention signed in Paris on 14th December 1960, and which came into force on 30th September 1961, the Organisation for Economic Co-operation and Development (OECD) shall promote policies designed:

- to achieve the highest sustainable economic growth and employment and a rising standard of living in Member countries, while maintaining financial stability, and thus to contribute to the development of the world economy;
- to contribute to sound economic expansion in Member as well as non-member countries in the process of economic development; and
- to contribute to the expansion of world trade on a multilateral, non-discriminatory basis in accordance with international obligations.

The original Member countries of the OECD are Austria, Belgium, Canada, Denmark, France, Germany, Greece, Iceland, Ireland, Italy, Luxembourg, the Netherlands, Norway, Portugal, Spain, Sweden, Switzerland, Turkey, the United Kingdom and the United States. The following countries became Members subsequently through accession at the dates indicated hereafter: Japan (28th April 1964), Finland (28th January 1969), Australia (7th June 1971), New Zealand (29th May 1973), Mexico (18th May 1994), the Czech Republic (21st December 1995), Hungary (7th May 1996), Poland (22nd November 1996) and Korea (12th December 1996). The Commission of the European Communities takes part in the work of the OECD (Article 13 of the OECD Convention).

In order to achieve its aims the OECD has set up a number of specialised committees. One of these is the Development Assistance Committee, whose Members have agreed to secure an expansion of aggregate volume of resources made available to developing countries and to improve their effectiveness. To this end, Members periodically review together both the amount and the nature of their contributions to aid programmes, bilateral and multilateral, and consult each other on all other relevant aspects of their development assistance policies.

The Members of the Development Assistance Committee are Australia, Austria, Belgium, Canada, Denmark, Finland, France, Germany, Ireland, Italy, Japan, Luxembourg, the Netherlands, New Zealand, Norway, Portugal, Spain, Sweden, Switzerland, the United Kingdom, the United States and the Commission of the European Communities.

Publié en français sous le titre :

SÉRIES DES EXAMENS EN MATIÈRE DE COOPÉRATION POUR LE DÉVELOPPEMENT
IRLANDE

Reprinted 1999

THE DEVELOPMENT ASSISTANCE COMMITTEE

Development Co-operation Review Series

HOW TO CONTACT US

The Development Assistance Committee welcomes your comments and suggestions.

Please contact us

by email at dac.contact@oecd.org, by telefax at 33 1 44 30 61 40
or by mail to:

Organisation for Economic Co-operation and Development
Development Co-operation Directorate
Communications and Management Support Unit
2, rue André-Pascal
75775 Paris Cedex 16
France

WORLD WIDE WEB SITE
http://www.oecd.org/dac

FOREWORD

The Development Assistance Committee (DAC) conducts periodic reviews to improve the individual and collective development co-operation efforts of DAC Members. The policies and efforts of individual Members are critically examined approximately once every three years. Some six programmes are examined annually.

The Peer Review is prepared by a team, consisting of representatives of the Secretariat working with officials from two DAC Members who are designated as examiners. The country under review provides a memorandum setting out the main developments in its policies and programmes. Then the Secretariat and the examiners visit the capital to interview officials, parliamentarians, and NGO representatives of the donor country to obtain a first-hand insight into current issues surrounding the development co-operation efforts of the Member concerned. Brief field visits investigate how Members have absorbed the major DAC policies, principles and concerns, and examine operations in recipient countries, particularly with regard to sustainability, gender equality and other aspects of participatory development, and local aid co-ordination.

Putting all this information and analysis together, the Secretariat prepares a draft report on the Member's development co-operation which is the basis for the DAC review meeting. At this meeting senior officials from the Member under review discuss a series of questions posed in a brief document: "Main Issues for the Review". These questions are formulated by the Secretariat in association with the examiners. The main discussion points and operational policy recommendations emerging from the review meeting are set out in the Summary and Conclusions section of the publication.

This publication contains the Summary and Conclusions as agreed by the Committee following its review on 21 June 1999 in Paris, and the Report prepared by the Secretariat in association with the examiners, representing Finland and Spain, on the development co-operation policies and efforts of Ireland. The report is published on the authority of the Secretary-General of the OECD.

Jean-Claude Faure
DAC Chairman

ACRONYMS

ADEA	Association for the Development of African Education
AfDB	African Development Bank
APSO	Agency for Personal Service Overseas
CGIAR	Consultative Group on International Agricultural Research
CRS	Creditor Reporting System
CSD	Commission on Sustainable Development
DAC	Development Assistance Committee
EBRD	European Bank for Reconstruction and Development
EC	European Community
ECHO	European Community Humanitarian Office
EDF	European Development Fund
EDI	Economic Development Institute
ESAF	Enhanced Structural Adjustment Facility
EU	European Union
EVP	European Volunteer Programme
FAO	Food and Agriculture Organization
GEF	Global Environment Fund
GNP	Gross national product
HIPC	Heavily-indebted poor countries
IAAC	Irish Aid Advisory Committee
IAEA	International Atomic Energy Agency
ICRC	International Commission of the Red Cross
IDA	International Development Association
IDC	Inter-Departmental Committee
IFAD	International Fund for Agricultural Development
IFC	International Financial Corporation
IFPA	Irish Family Planning Association
ILO	International Labour Organization
IMF	International Monetary Fund
ICRC	International Committee of the Red Cross
JSC	Joint Standing Committee
MORI	Market and Opinion Research International
NCDE	National Committee for Development Education

NGOs	Non-governmental organisations
OA	Official aid
ODA	Official development assistance
PAC	Preliminary Appraisal Committee
PAEG	Projects Appraisal and Evaluation Group
SADC	Southern African Development Community
SMI	Strategic Management Initiative
SWAps	Sector-wide approaches
UN	United Nations
UNCED	United Nations Conference on Environment and Development
UNCSD	United Nations Commission on Sustainable Development
UNDP	United Nations Development Programme
UNEP	United Nations Environment Programme
UNESCO	United Nations Educational, Scientific and Cultural Organization
UNFPA	United Nations Fund for Population Activities
UNHCR	United Nations High Commission for Refugees
UNICEF	United Nations Children's Fund
UNITAR	United Nations Institute for Training and Research
UNV	United Nations Volunteers
UPU	Universal Postal Union
WFP	World Food Programme
WID	Women in development
WIPO	World Intellectual Property Organization
WHO	World Health Organization
WMO	World Meteorological Organization
WTO	World Trade Organization

Exchange rates (Ir£ per $) were:

1993	1994	1995	1996	1997	1998
0.6833	0.6697	0.6245	0.6254	0.6604	0.7030

Signs used:

()	Secretariat estimate in whole or part
-	Nil
0.0	Negligible
..	Not available
...	Not available separately but included in total
n.a.	Not applicable
P	Provisional

Slight discrepancies in totals are due to rounding

Ireland's aid at a glance

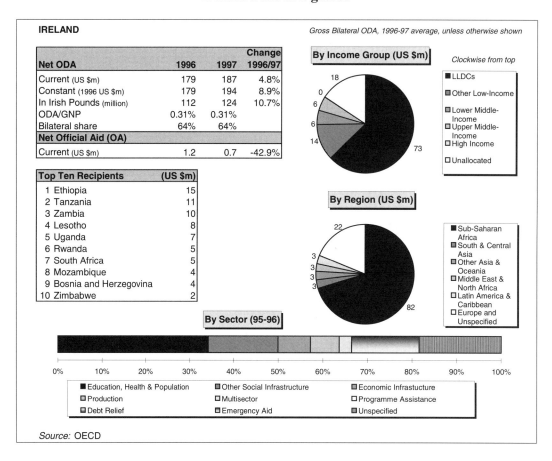

IRELAND

Gross Bilateral ODA, 1996-97 average, unless otherwise shown

Net ODA	1996	1997	Change 1996/97
Current (US $m)	179	187	4.8%
Constant (1996 US $m)	179	194	8.9%
In Irish Pounds (million)	112	124	10.7%
ODA/GNP	0.31%	0.31%	
Bilateral share	64%	64%	
Net Official Aid (OA)			
Current (US $m)	1.2	0.7	-42.9%

Top Ten Recipients	(US $m)
1 Ethiopia	15
2 Tanzania	11
3 Zambia	10
4 Lesotho	8
5 Uganda	7
6 Rwanda	5
7 South Africa	5
8 Mozambique	4
9 Bosnia and Herzegovina	4
10 Zimbabwe	2

By Income Group (US $m)

Clockwise from top

- ■ LLDCs
- ▨ Other Low-Income
- ▨ Lower Middle-Income
- ▨ Upper Middle-Income
- □ High Income
- □ Unallocated

18, 0, 6, 6, 14, 73

By Region (US $m)

- ■ Sub-Saharan Africa
- ▨ South & Central Asia
- ▨ Other Asia & Oceania
- ▨ Middle East & North Africa
- □ Latin America & Caribbean
- □ Europe and Unspecified

22, 3, 3, 3, 3, 82

By Sector (95-96)

0% 10% 20% 30% 40% 50% 60% 70% 80% 90% 100%

- ■ Education, Health & Population
- ▨ Other Social Infrastructure
- ▨ Economic Infrastucture
- □ Production
- □ Multisector
- □ Programme Assistance
- ▨ Debt Relief
- ▨ Emergency Aid
- ▨ Unspecified

Source: OECD

TABLE OF CONTENTS

Tables

Charts

Figures

Boxes

SUMMARY AND CONCLUSIONS

Irish Aid today sets high standards for the official aid programme. The programme is growing and is expected to continue to do so, as a reflection of Ireland's commitment to reducing poverty in developing countries, and of Ireland's place in the world. Ireland's potential for further growth in aid is supported by a strong economic performance, coupled with solid political and public support for development co-operation in general. Ireland's experience as a recipient of Structural and Cohesion Funds from the European Union (EU) has demonstrated to the Irish that aid can work.

In 1999 Irish Aid celebrates the 25th anniversary of the establishment of the official aid programme. After six years of impressive growth in volume and improvement in quality, most of the increase in aid in 1999 is being used for debt relief measures, EU contributions, emergency humanitarian assistance and support for refugees in Ireland, rather than for allocations for the long-term development programmes administered by the Department of Foreign Affairs. Political commitments on aid allocations undertaken by the Minister of Finance mean that increases in the Department of Foreign Affairs' part of the programme are now expected in 2000 and 2001.

Two main issues confront the Irish Aid programme: how best to grow and how best to manage that growth. These are clearly issues which Ireland needs to consider and resolve itself but the Development Assistance Committee (DAC) can draw on its collective experience to contribute to Ireland's reflections on these issues. A starting point, from experience elsewhere, is that Irish Aid should maintain and enhance the focused nature of the programme which is now one of its major strengths.

A strong policy basis

Ireland sees development co-operation as an integral part of its foreign relations and has built up a strong policy basis which serves as a guiding strategy for the Irish Aid programme. This policy basis draws on the long Irish tradition of direct contacts with developing countries, in particular through missionary activities and the work of non-governmental organisations (NGOs). At the same time, the Irish programme is a good reflection of current international policy orientations aimed at eradicating poverty and promoting sustainable people-centred development in partnership with developing countries. Irish Aid's policies were fleshed out in *Irish Aid: Consolidation and Growth – A Strategy Plan* (July 1993) and were further developed in the government's 1996 White Paper on Foreign Policy *Challenges and Opportunities Abroad*. They are implemented with the guidance provided by the Department of Foreign Affairs' annual strategy statements.

Ireland has worked out good systems for promoting coherence in its policies which impact on developing countries, as well as among its various channels for delivering aid. The DAC encourages Ireland to pursue its leadership in this area.

The mission of Irish Aid is to contribute to Ireland's broader efforts to achieve the overall goals of international peace, security and a just and stable global economic system. Recognising that

13

development can only take place when local people are fully involved through a democratic and inclusive process, Irish Aid is supporting decentralisation and local government structures in many parts of its programme.

Ireland's aid programme is consistent with the orientations agreed upon by DAC Members in 1996 in *Shaping the 21st Century Strategy: The Contribution of Development Co-operation*:

- Ireland is expanding its **resources for development co-operation**.

- The programme has a **poverty reduction** focus, concentrating not just on least-developed countries but on poor regions within those countries, in a partnership approach.

- Irish Aid is oriented towards the social sector and, increasingly, towards support for **basic health** and **basic education**, although the focus could be sharpened.

- Efforts are being made to mainstream **gender** concerns throughout the programme.

- **Environmental sustainability** is being more systematically addressed and additional resources have been provided to support activities in the environment area.

- **Human rights and democratisation** activities are integrated into priority country programmes while in other countries specific actions are funded through a special fund.

Putting partnerships into practice

Irish Aid is a strong performer in putting a partnerships approach into practice, especially in the six least-developed countries in sub-Saharan Africa where the bilateral programme is concentrated: Ethiopia, Lesotho, Mozambique, Tanzania, Uganda and Zambia. Irish Aid recognises the need for developing country (and local) ownership of the aid process, and carries out its programmes in partnership with recipient governments and people, and in line with their priorities. While continuing to target its assistance at local or district level through its area-based programmes, Irish Aid is becoming more involved at the national level, through programme aid and support for selected sector-wide approaches. As a small donor, Irish Aid does its full part to co-operate and co-ordinate with other donors in its areas of concentration to enhance the collective impact of aid programmes. In its priority countries, Irish Aid has the potential to play a more significant role in co-ordination activities at the national level to share with other donors the benefit of its experience.

Ireland's partnership approach was apparent during a field visit to Uganda in preparation for this review. Ireland has been implementing an area-based programme in the District of Kibaale since 1995. In this district, Ireland works through local structures, building local capacity and institutions in support of locally-defined priorities. Taking a flexible approach has paid off by helping to establish a strong development partnership and laying the foundations for subsequent work. At the same time, Irish Aid works to support the national poverty reduction strategy as well as Ugandan-led work on sector-wide programmes in health and education.

Ireland's growing aid programme

Successive government commitments during the 1990s to expand Ireland's official development assistance (ODA) have had the goal of bringing Ireland's aid performance in line with that of its European partners and, ultimately, meet the United Nations (UN) target for ODA of 0.7 per cent of gross national product (GNP). In its *Programme for Partnership Government*, the coalition government formed after elections in 1992 pledged to increase Ireland's ODA to 0.40 per cent of GNP by 1997. The present Irish government's *Action Plan for the Millennium* includes the commitment to increase allocations for ODA to 0.45 per cent of GNP by 2002.

These commitments have resulted in steady and substantial increases in the volume of Irish ODA, although the stated ODA/GNP objectives have not yet been achieved. Between 1992 and 1998, Irish ODA trebled, rising from $70 million (Ir£ 40 million) to a provisional $199 million (Ir£ 140 million), while performance in relation to a growing GNP almost doubled, rising from 0.16 per cent to 0.30 per cent, and is projected to reach 0.35 per cent in 1999. Starting from a low base, the main official programme administered by the Department of Foreign Affairs' Development Co-operation Division increased more than fourfold.

The last DAC review and the present one have traced the impressive process through which Irish Aid has managed to accomplish such volume increases, while simultaneously strengthening the quality and operating professionalism of the programme. By any comparative standard, this record of successfully combining volume growth with improving quality would unquestionably justify further increases in Irish aid. The growth to date has had to be arranged, however, without the necessary strengthening of staffing levels and administrative systems for the Development Co-operation Division. DAC comparative experience suggests that the division's capacity to manage the programme is at this stage stretched, dependent on a few key individuals and thus highly vulnerable. This review has thus ranked these organisational and staffing requirements as key for the Irish authorities.

Following Ireland's entry into the European Economic and Monetary Union on 1 January 1999, and the fixing of official interest rates in Ireland by the European Central Bank, the Irish government has focussed on restricting public expenditures to contain inflationary pressures. Budget allocations in 1999 for long-term development programmes were thus almost unchanged from their 1998 level. However, a Cabinet-level agreement was worked out with a commitment to increase the department's aid allocation from Ir£110 million (140 million euro) in 1999 to at least Ir£136 million (173 million euro) in 2000 and Ir£159 million (202 million euro) in 2001. This provides Irish Aid, for the first time, with a firm multi-annual budget which offers the potential to improve management of the programme, assuming that the issue of management resources is also met.

Organisational structure of Ireland's aid programme

Two major and three smaller organisations, all under the responsibility of the Minister of Foreign Affairs, are associated with the delivery of Ireland's ODA:

- The **Development Co-operation Division** of the Department of Foreign Affairs plays the central role in managing and co-ordinating Ireland's development co-operation. It administers six priority country programmes, projects in "other bilateral" countries and the NGO Schemes and special funds. It is also responsible for Ireland's multilateral assistance through the EU development programmes and voluntary contributions to UN development and relief agencies and funds.

- The **Agency for Personal Service Overseas** (APSO) is an independent, state-sponsored body which promotes temporary volunteer service in developing countries, both directly and through co-funding with NGOs. APSO's programme is concentrated in 16 priority countries, in Africa, Central America and now Cambodia. In 1998, APSO funded 1 261 development workers in 84 countries, on both short- and long-term assignments.

- The **Irish Council for Overseas Students** assists with the administration of Irish Aid's Fellowship Programme which provides tertiary scholarships and support services for people from developing countries, usually for study in Ireland.

- The **National Committee for Development Education** (NCDE) is a consultative body which encourages and supports development education in all sectors of Irish society.

- The **Refugee Agency** is a non-statutory body which co-ordinates the admission, reception and resettlement of programme refugees admitted to Ireland, with some parts of its budget being claimed as ODA.

Eight other government departments are involved in Ireland's national effort in support of development co-operation. The Department of Finance has primary responsibility for Ireland's relations with the World Bank Group, including the International Development Association (IDA), the International Monetary Fund (IMF) and the European Bank for Reconstruction and Development (EBRD). Other departments -- including those of Agriculture and Food; Health and Children; Enterprise, Trade and Development; and Environment and Local Government -- also contribute through their participation in and funding for relevant multilateral agencies.

Partly due to the relatively small size of Ireland's government and aid programme, informal co-ordination between these various departments can still work effectively, enabling Ireland to achieve a good degree of coherence in most of its policies towards developing countries. At a more formal level, mechanisms exist for collaboration on the implementation of bilateral and multilateral programmes, while co-ordination with other agencies and channels remains more informal.

An objective stated in *Promoting Ireland's Interests: Strategy Statement of the Department of Foreign Affairs 1998-2000* is to strengthen the management of Irish Aid by increasing the coherence and synergies between the various organisations involved in the delivery of Irish Aid. It appears that much can be done to achieve this objective. Integration of APSO with the main programme managed by the Development Co-operation Division is one option which could be explored. As a minimum, closer co-ordination between APSO and the Department of Foreign Affairs is needed, especially in Lesotho, Tanzania, Uganda and Zambia which are priority countries for both programmes.

In 1999 as Ireland celebrates the 25th anniversary of its official aid programme, a special statement of national commitment to promoting development and reducing poverty in developing countries as priority goals for all government policy could strengthen awareness of what has been achieved and help consolidate public and political support for further challenges.

How best to grow

The prospect for growth in the Irish Aid budget is particularly welcome since Ireland, like other donors, is expected to need to contribute to debt relief and to emerging demands for major relief and reconstruction programmes. It will be a great advantage if Ireland is enabled to respond to such demands without diverting resources from its long-term development programmes. Building on its existing strengths, Irish Aid has several options for channelling additional ODA funding. These include:

- Intensifying existing priority country programmes.

- Launching new priority country programmes.

- Starting different types of bilateral activities.

- Increasing funding for NGO Schemes and special funds.

- Expanding contributions to multilateral agencies.

Various combinations of these options could be used. However, if Ireland is to maintain its clear strategic objectives and its performance in implementing them, decisions should be based on development criteria and the scope for Irish impacts on poverty reduction. Drawing on lessons of other DAC programmes that have grown quickly, Irish Aid should not become dispersed, nor overlook the staffing and management demands entailed by different options for expansion.

Irish Aid: Consolidation and Growth provided excellent guidance for how Ireland's aid programme should expand during the period 1993 to 1997. This was backed by the strong political commitment contained in the *Programme for a Partnership Government*. To steer growth in the programme up to 2002 and beyond, Ireland could usefully consider producing a written implementation programme by up-dating *Irish Aid: Consolidation and Growth*, spelling out how further expansion in Irish Aid will be achieved.

Intensifying existing priority country programmes

One important option is to invest more in Irish Aid's six priority country programmes where local circumstances allow. These programmes absorbed 29 per cent of total ODA in 1997 but Ireland is still a small donor in these countries -- in 1997, Irish ODA ranged from 0.6 per cent of total receipts from all sources in Mozambique to 5.3 per cent in Lesotho. There is thus clearly room for Ireland to build on its strong base and become a less marginal actor in these countries. Some of the trends already underway in the priority country programmes -- growth and new activities in sectoral and programme aid -- could lead to an expansion, intensification of the benefits of country concentration and higher quality. Nevertheless, it should not be assumed that these trends will automatically lead to rapid expansion of disbursements.

Launching new priority country programmes

Another option for Ireland is to consider starting priority country programmes in new countries. However, there are no strong imperatives for Ireland to pursue these dispersion options that might exist for other donors, for example for historical, geographic or commercial reasons. This freedom to concentrate is a considerable and enviable advantage for the Irish programme. If it wishes to maintain its special strengths, and avoid some common pitfalls, Irish Aid should consequently evaluate carefully even a modest extension of the programme to new countries based on the expectation of additional resources being available over the next two years.

Starting different types of bilateral activities

Irish Aid's priority countries are located in Eastern and Southern Africa. This gives Ireland a good basis for developing regional programmes in these areas and providing support for regional institutions, such as the Southern African Development Community (SADC). Conceivably, Ireland could intensify its programmes in other countries in these regions where it already has some contacts, familiarity and experience, such as Eritrea, Malawi, Namibia, Rwanda and Zimbabwe. As has been done in Nigeria and South Africa, upgrading the programmes in these countries need not necessarily imply establishing full priority country programmes.

Technical assistance from Ireland related to its experience with successfully attracting foreign direct investment and managing well external financing for development purposes (Structural and Cohesion Funds from the EU) might possibly be useful to a good number of developing countries.

Increasing funding for NGO Schemes and special funds

Ireland's national effort includes the continuing work of Irish NGOs, some with strong international reputations and high profiles at home. By DAC standards, direct support for NGO activities and support through NGOs already absorbs a relatively large share of the Irish government's aid spending (in total, nearly one quarter of Ireland's ODA in 1997). Moreover, Irish NGOs are generously supported by the Irish public and receive funding from other sources, such as the EU and United Nations agencies. Therefore, the option of increasing the amount of aid channelled through NGOs would not appear to be an obvious choice for disbursing substantial amounts of additional funds.

Many observers, including NGOs themselves, are sceptical about large increases in funding levels, as it is doubtful whether Irish NGOs could expand their programmes more than marginally, at least in the short-term, and maintain quality in their activities. Irish Aid is already funding the majority of applications it receives for its NGO Co-Financing Scheme and so it is not apparent that a sufficient flow of high quality projects currently exists to justify additional funding. Additional funding channelled through NGOs could, however, be directed towards indigenous organisations in developing countries, such as by expanding the In-Country Micro Project Scheme, especially in Irish Aid's priority and "other bilateral" countries. There would also be merit in reinforcing the development potential in these "other bilateral" programmes by expanding activities through the Human Rights and Democratisation Programme in these countries.

Expanding contributions to multilateral agencies

In addition to Ireland's assessed contributions to multilateral agencies, its voluntary contributions have increased fourfold since 1992. Their allocation in 1997 amounted to 6 per cent of ODA. Ireland has a lively and active engagement multilaterally and provides voluntary contributions to an increasingly large number of UN agencies — some 39 agencies in 1999 -- although most support continues to be directed to the United Nations Development Programme (UNDP), the United Nations Children's Fund (UNICEF) and the United Nations High Commission for Refugees (UNHCR).

An option for channelling additional aid funds is to adopt a more selective and targeted approach to increasing voluntary contributions to multilateral agencies which reinforce Irish Aid's policy objectives, in particular its poverty reduction focus. As in its priority countries, Ireland might benefit from becoming less of a marginal player in some of the multilateral agencies it supports.

There would now appear to be a strong case for Ireland to join the African Development Bank (AfDB) and this is under consideration. The budget is available and most analyses confirm that the Bank's reforms and programme directions merit support. Membership would be another means for Ireland to maintain and enhance the focussed nature of its programme and to bring its experience from working in some of the poorest countries in Africa to discussions at the Bank. Joining the AfDB would also have the indirect benefit of opening up to Irish firms the possibility of tendering for AfDB projects and procurement.

Debt relief

The issue of contributing to the relief of the debt burden of developing countries has been the subject of lively debate in Ireland. Like other DAC Members, Ireland has acknowledged that, for a number of highly-indebted poor countries, successful development co-operation will also depend upon concerted international action to alleviate an unsustainable debt burden.

All Irish ODA is in grant form and developing countries have no outstanding official debts to Ireland. Nonetheless, Ireland has adopted a policy advocating debt relief and in September 1998 announced its willingness to participate in debt relief measures, agreeing to provide a total of Ir£ 31.5 million (40.0 million euro) over 12 years to assist the most heavily-indebted poor countries (HIPC). From this package of bilateral and multilateral measures, Ir£ 17.0 million (21.6 million euro) is being disbursed in 1999, 11 per cent of aid allocations for this year. Ireland is also looking carefully at current international initiatives aimed at deepening and broadening the scope of the HIPC initiative and speeding up disbursements. While these debt relief efforts will contribute to resolving an urgent problem in the short term, they should not be expected to be a continuing growth area for the Irish Aid programme.

How best to manage growth in the aid programme

Managing growth in aid volume

Many DAC Members have seen their aid programmes grow, or decline, rapidly. One lesson that can be drawn from these experiences is that growth which is too rapid or too erratic is destabilising for the long-term efforts of an aid agency and can jeopardise aid quality and effectiveness, and thus the value of the aid programme. Managing a sustained and significant increase in aid well requires setting an orderly growth path, with a clear target, and milestones along the way. A donor should also ensure that an expanding programme continues to draw upon and reinforce its comparative advantages and experience, along with its staffing and organisation.

Managing increased aid volume

While there are clearly competing demands for limited public resources in Ireland, the internationally-recognised quality of Ireland's aid programme now justifies a strong claim for continued increases in funding. The Minister of Finance's commitment to increase allocations for the Department of Foreign Affairs provides Irish Aid with an orderly growth path for 2000 and 2001. The Irish government also remains committed to reaching a GNP target of 0.45 per cent in 2002 for the ODA programme as a whole. Following the budget discussions in 1998, it will be important for the longer-term growth path and milestones to be clarified as much as possible.

Human resources

The number and skill mix of staff currently available to manage the Irish Aid programme as well as staffing regulations are widely seen as inadequate. They must be reinforced and changed if Ireland's contribution to development co-operation is to be maintained and further enhanced. It is critical that the review commissioned in 1999 of the adequacy of the Department of Foreign Affairs' existing management resources results in the provision of the additional staff which Irish Aid needs.

To manage Irish Aid's growing programme, the Development Co-operation Division has had to improvise and patch together temporary ways of reinforcing staff capacities, in Dublin and in the field, within complex government staffing regulations. With a total staff of 82 people in 1999, the division is stretched and its structure fragile. Constraints on staff mobility and administrative obstacles limit the division's capacity to manage and deploy its staff optimally and to offer career possibilities for all its staff. The division and embassies in priority countries are managed by career diplomats, on rotations of two-to-four years' duration. In Dublin, these people are supported by general service staff, mainly in administrative and support positions, and specialists on two-year renewable contracts. Neither of these latter groups can serve overseas. In priority countries, the programmes are administered by programme officers, on two-year renewable contracts for up to a maximum of five years in any one country, who cannot be redeployed to Dublin. In Irish Aid's structure, only diplomatic staff at the first secretary level can serve both in Dublin and in the field. The Irish Aid system is thus vulnerable as within just a few years many, and potentially all, of Irish Aid's current staff will have moved on or been redeployed to another part of the department. Institutional memory and operational expertise will be lost in this process.

If the current organisational structure is maintained, several changes could be considered to improve performance. One suggestion is to structure a development specialisation within the diplomatic stream which could lead to the highest positions within the Department of Foreign Affairs. This would involve ensuring that most levels of diplomatic staff are represented both in Dublin and in the field. Representation in some of the priority countries could be up-graded to full ambassador status or an ambassador with regional responsibilities for development co-operation could be placed in the field. Where ambassadors are stationed in developing countries, they should be supported by junior diplomats, in programme administration roles.

Creating a core-group of competent, specialised contract staff is crucial for Irish Aid. For contract staff, the present two-year duration appears unnecessarily cautious and Irish Aid would improve staff motivation and commitment through longer contracts, particularly for those with proven capacity. More general selection criteria and job descriptions could be used to recruit contract staff, enabling those who so wished to be subsequently redeployed, thus increasing interchange between Dublin and the field. The situation of programme officers merits particular attention. Programme officers play a pivotal role in the management of Irish Aid's programmes in the field. Several are now reaching their five-year limit. Current policy would require their contracts not be renewed, if it is not possible to transfer them to another posting, which would be detrimental.

Possible organisational options for Ireland's aid programme

For the short- to medium-term, through a period of consolidation, reinforcing the existing organisation by all means described above would seem to be the preferable option.

In the longer-term, planning and assessment can be carried out on other possible options, of which three seem most plausible, on the basis of comparable experience:

- Maintain the improved *status quo* arrangements outlined above.

- Establish an independent implementing agency for the bilateral programme.

- Create a fully-integrated, geographically-based Department of Foreign Affairs.

Establishing an independent implementing agency

This option is probably the most appealing from an operational point of view. The Department of Foreign Affairs would maintain overall political responsibility for the programme as a whole, as well as specific responsibility for multilateral assistance, bilateral aid policy and secretariat and liaison functions for associated bodies, such as the Irish Aid Advisory Committee. An implementing agency could be established as an independent state-sponsored body, which would allow greater flexibility in staffing matters while offering staff greater employment stability and improved career prospects.

Creating an integrated Department of Foreign Affairs

Another option might be to "de-compartmentalise" development co-operation within the Department of Foreign Affairs by creating integrated regional/country desks to take responsibility for all aspects of Ireland's bilateral relations: foreign policy, trade and, in the case of relations with developing countries, development co-operation. This has been done in some other DAC Member countries. It would not appear, however, to be a preferable option in view of the size of Ireland's Department of Foreign Affairs and the dilution of aid experience this option would entail.

Evaluation and aid effectiveness

Irish Aid's Evaluation and Audit Unit has been separated from the specialist programme support activities and now reports directly to the head of the Development Co-operation Division. Despite its small size, the unit is active, carrying out evaluations of individual projects, country programmes and particular sectors as well as participating in joint donor exercises and working with associated Irish Aid bodies, such as APSO. Evaluations are, in principle, available to the public although details of evaluations undertaken are not well known. Starting with 1998, the list of evaluations carried out each year is published in the Irish Aid annual report and the executive summaries of completed evaluations will be available on Irish Aid's Internet site[1], thus enhancing public accountability.

The value of *ex post* evaluations is diminished when staff turnover is rapid, as those people most associated with the project evaluated will have moved on. It is more important, therefore, for Irish Aid to promote a culture of evaluation whereby operational staff are continuously involved in monitoring performance and conducting self-evaluations of programmes and projects. The field visit to Uganda found that Irish Aid could still do more to engender a culture of evaluation and a focus on monitoring and results. Moreover, Ireland's present evaluation plan currently focuses on sector and thematic evaluations, and not on area-based programmes. The evaluation of area-based programmes should be given greater emphasis.

---

1.   The address of Irish Aid's Internet site is: *http://www.irlgov.ie/iveagh*

Summary of main recommendations:

1. A written implementation programme up-dating *Irish Aid: Consolidation and Growth* would give clear direction for future growth in the aid programme.

2. To mark Irish Aid's 25th anniversary, Ireland should renew its commitment to promoting development and reducing poverty as priority goals for all government policy.

3. Decisions on expansion of the programme should be based on development criteria and the scope for Irish impacts on poverty reduction.

4. Irish Aid should maintain and enhance its focused nature. Even a modest extension in the number of priority countries should be evaluated carefully.

5. Ireland should pursue its consideration of joining the African Development Bank.

6. Staffing, skill mixes and career perspectives must be reinforced and changed if Ireland's contribution to development co-operation is to be maintained and further enhanced.

7. Reinforcing existing organisational structures is preferable in the short-term. In the longer-term, establishing an independent implementing agency is an appealing option from an operational point of view.

8. Irish Aid could do more to engender a culture of evaluation and a focus on monitoring and results. The evaluation of area-based programmes should be given greater emphasis.

CHAPTER 1

IRELAND'S EXPANDING AID PROGRAMME

Strong political and public support in Ireland for development co-operation has provided the foundations for an expansion and renewal of Ireland's development co-operation programme during the 1990s. The political impetus for sustained growth in Ireland's aid volume was provided in *Programme for a Partnership Government*, the policy framework agreement of the Irish coalition government formed after elections in 1992. This agreement reaffirmed Ireland's commitment to the millions of people in danger of death from drought, famine and disease or who are living in poverty and social and economic deprivation. It re-established aid as a prominent issue for the Irish government by pledging to increase official development assistance (ODA) to a level of 0.4 per cent of gross national product (GNP) by 1997. It envisaged achieving this expansion by extending the number of bilateral priority country programmes beyond the four then in operation, by further developing training and tertiary scholarship activities and by mandating the Agency for Personal Service Overseas (APSO) to quadruple the number of Irish volunteers on assignment in developing countries, to 2 000 by 1997.

Further guidance on orientations and objectives for Irish Aid -- Ireland's official development co-operation programme -- has been provided and developed through a series of policy and strategy documents, prepared by the Department of Foreign Affairs after consultations with the public and prominent members of the development community in Ireland. *Irish Aid: Consolidation and Growth -- A Strategy Plan* (July 1993) spelt out, for the period 1993 to 1997, the ways in which an expanded programme could provide greater assistance and give economic and technical support to people in developing countries. These orientations were further refined, within the broader context of Ireland's overall foreign policy relations, in *Challenges and Opportunities Abroad: White Paper on Foreign Policy* (1996). Implementation of these policies is being guided by *Pursuing Ireland's External Interests: Strategy Statement of the Department of Foreign Affairs* (March 1997) and *Promoting Ireland's Interests: Strategy Statement of the Department of Foreign Affairs, 1998-2000* (1998).

These four documents constitute a solid policy basis for the aid programme. They provide a good reflection of current international policy orientations aimed at eradicating poverty and promoting sustainable people-centred development in partnership with developing countries. They are consistent with the orientations agreed upon by Members of the Development Assistance Committee (DAC) in 1996 in *Shaping the 21st Century Strategy: The Contribution of Development Co-operation*. At the same time, and as discussed in Chapter 2, there would be some merit in summarising the main thrust of Irish Aid's policies in a succinct consolidated statement.

Overview of Ireland's aid programme

Ireland's ODA programme is the third smallest among the 21 DAC Member countries but distinguishes itself by the focussed nature which constitutes one of its major strengths. It is estimated that around one third of Irish ODA is spent on basic social sectors. All Irish ODA is provided in grant form.

Irish Aid's bilateral programme focuses on six least-developed countries in sub-Saharan Africa: Ethiopia, Lesotho, Mozambique, Tanzania, Uganda and Zambia. These priority country programmes absorbed 29 per cent of total Irish ODA in 1997. These programmes are supplemented by smaller "other bilateral" programmes in a range of countries — currently Bangladesh, Cambodia, Ghana, Malawi, Namibia, the Palestinian Administered Areas, South Africa, Sudan, Viet Nam and Zimbabwe — which received 4 per cent of total ODA. Irish Aid's strong commitment to human rights, democratisation and improving basic social services -- particularly water and sanitation, food security, health and education -- is particularly apparent in these programmes.

Irish Aid funds three schemes which provide support to non-governmental organisations (NGOs). The Block Grant Scheme provides support for five large Irish NGOs. The Co-financing Scheme finances individual development projects. The In-country Micro Projects Scheme provides support through indigenous NGOs for local project activities. Collectively, these schemes received 6 per cent of funding in 1997. Three other programmes are channelled through NGOs or international agencies, or are provided directly to recipient countries. These are the Emergency Humanitarian Assistance Fund, the Emergency Preparedness and Post-Emergency Rehabilitation Fund and the Human Rights and Democratisation Programme. Together these accounted for another 9 per cent of Ireland's ODA.

Ireland's bilateral aid also supports the co-financing of activities with multilateral agencies (2 per cent of total ODA) and training and scholarships for tertiary studies, usually in Ireland (1 per cent of ODA).

Ireland has a volunteer programme funded by Irish Aid but managed by APSO. It absorbed a further 9 per cent of ODA. APSO's programme focuses on 16 priority countries.

Ireland's multilateral assistance comprises aid channelled through European Union (EU) development programmes (21 per cent of total ODA in 1997) and mandatory subscriptions (8 per cent of ODA) and voluntary contributions (6 per cent of ODA) to a range of international financial institutions and United Nations (UN) development and relief agencies and funds. Voluntary contributions support an increasingly large number of UN agencies and funds — a total of 39 in 1999, including a number of token contributions. Among the development banks, Ireland is a member of the World Bank and European Bank for Reconstruction and Development (EBRD) but is not a member of any of the regional development banks whose activities primarily favour developing countries.

In recent years, Ireland has been moving towards more programme and sector aid in its priority country programmes, as well as support for bilateral and multilateral debt relief packages, such as the heavily-indebted poor countries (HIPC) initiative.

Outlook for Ireland's aid volume

Successive government commitments during the 1990s to expand Ireland's ODA have had the goal of bringing Ireland's aid performance in line with that of its European partners and, ultimately, of meeting the UN target for ODA of 0.7 per cent of GNP. These commitments have resulted in steady and substantial increases in the volume of Irish ODA. Between 1992 and 1998, Irish ODA trebled, rising from $70 million (Ir£40 million) to a provisional $199 million (Ir£140 million). However, due to a rapidly growing economy, Ireland did not meet its 1997 target for ODA (0.4 per cent of GNP) even though its ODA/GNP ratio did almost double from 0.16 per cent in 1992 to 0.31 per cent in 1996 and 1997, before declining to 0.30 per cent in 1998.

With Ireland's entry into the European Economic and Monetary Union on 1 January 1999, official interest rates in Ireland are now those fixed by the European Central Bank for the 11 euro countries combined. As Ireland is no longer able to set interest rates high to contain inflationary pressures, the Irish government has focussed on restricting public expenditures.

It was in this context that budget allocations in 1999 for long-term development programmes administered by the Department of Foreign Affairs were almost unchanged from their 1998 level (additional allocations for aid in 1999 were used to fund debt relief measures, EU contributions, emergency humanitarian assistance and support for refugees in Ireland). The Minister of State responsible for development co-operation took a strong public stance against this decision and, in response, a cabinet-level agreement was worked out which included a commitment to increase the department's aid allocation from Ir£110 million (140 million euro) in 1999 to at least Ir£136 million (173 million euro) in 2000 and Ir£159 million (202 million euro) in 2001.

Based on conservative estimates for the other parts of the ODA programme, Irish Aid predicts that total ODA could rise from Ir£178 million (226 million euro) in 1999 to at least Ir£186 million (236 million euro) in 2000 and Ir£210 million (267 million euro) in 2001. Current trends in GNP growth would imply that Ireland's ODA/GNP ratio could reach 0.35 per cent in 1999 and 2000, and 0.37 per cent in 2001.

The present Irish government's *Action Plan for the Millennium* includes the commitment to increase allocations for ODA to 0.45 per cent of GNP by 2002. Achieving this target may well require even more substantial increases in allocations for ODA than currently envisaged.

Irish Aid consequently has good reasons to expect its budget allocations to continue expanding. This raises the issue of how best to use these additional funds.

How best to grow

The prospect for growth in the Irish Aid budget is particularly welcome since Ireland, like other donors, is expected to need to contribute to debt relief and to emerging demands for major relief and reconstruction programmes. It will be a great advantage if Ireland is enabled to respond to such demands without diverting resources from its long-term development programmes. Building on its existing strengths, Irish Aid has several options for channelling additional ODA funding. These include:

- Intensifying existing priority country programmes.

- Launching new priority country programmes.

- Starting different types of bilateral activities.

- Increasing funding for NGO Schemes and special funds.

- Expanding contributions to multilateral agencies.

Various combinations of these options could be used. However, if Ireland is to maintain its clear strategic objectives and its performance in implementing them, decisions should be based on development criteria and the scope for Irish impacts on poverty reduction. Drawing on lessons of other DAC programmes that have grown quickly, Irish Aid should not become dispersed, nor overlook the staffing and management demands entailed by different options for expansion.

Intensifying existing priority country programmes

One important option is to invest more in Irish Aid's six priority country programmes where local circumstances allow. Ireland is still a small donor in these countries -- in 1997, its contributions ranged from 0.6 per cent of total receipts from all sources in Mozambique to 5.3 per cent in Lesotho. There is thus clearly room for Ireland to build on its strong base and become a less marginal actor in these countries. Some of the trends already underway in the priority country programmes -- growth and new activities in sectoral and programme aid -- could lead to an expansion, intensification of the benefits of country concentration and higher quality. Nevertheless, it should not be assumed that these trends will automatically lead to rapid expansion of disbursements.

Launching new priority country programmes

Another option for Ireland is to consider starting priority country programmes in new countries, as was done when the programme first started expanding in 1993. However, there are no strong imperatives for Ireland to pursue these dispersion options that might exist for other donors, for example for historical, geographic or commercial reasons. This freedom to concentrate is a considerable and enviable advantage for the Irish programme. If it wishes to maintain its special strengths, and avoid some common pitfalls, Irish Aid should consequently evaluate carefully even a modest extension of the programme to new countries based on the expectation of additional resources being available over the next two years.

Starting different types of bilateral activities

Irish Aid's priority countries are located in Eastern and Southern Africa. This gives Ireland a good basis for developing regional programmes in these areas and providing support for regional institutions, such as the Southern African Development Community (SADC). Conceivably, Ireland could intensify its programmes in other countries in these regions where it already has some contacts, familiarity and experience, such as Eritrea, Malawi, Namibia, Rwanda and Zimbabwe. As has been done in Nigeria and South Africa, upgrading the programmes in these countries need not necessarily imply establishing full priority country programmes and opening a large field office.

Technical assistance from Ireland related to its experience with successfully attracting foreign direct investment and managing well external financing for development purposes (Structural and Cohesion Funds from the EU) might possibly be useful to a good number of developing countries.

Increasing funding for NGO Schemes and special funds

Ireland's national effort includes the continuing work of Irish NGOs, some with strong international reputations and high profiles at home. By DAC standards, direct support for NGO activities and support through NGOs already absorbs a relatively large share of the Irish government's aid spending. Moreover, Irish NGOs are generously supported by the Irish public and receive funding from other sources, such as the EU and UN agencies. While the option of increasing the amount of aid channelled through NGOs is a possibility, this would not appear to be an obvious choice at this time for disbursing substantial amounts of additional funds.

Many observers, including NGOs themselves, are sceptical about large increases in funding, as it is doubtful whether Irish NGOs could expand their programmes more than marginally, at least in the short-term, and maintain quality in their activities. Irish Aid funds the majority of applications it receives for its NGO Co-Financing Scheme and so it is not apparent that a sufficient flow of high quality projects currently exists to justify additional funding. Moreover, it should be remembered that NGO activities are not restricted to Irish Aid's priority countries and increased aid through NGOs would result in greater geographical dispersion of Ireland's ODA. Additional funding channelled through NGOs could, however, be directed towards indigenous organisations in developing countries, such as by expanding the In-Country Micro Project Scheme, especially in Irish Aid's priority and "other bilateral" countries. There would also be merit in reinforcing the development potential in these "other bilateral" programmes by expanding activities through the Human Rights and Democratisation Programme in these countries.

Expanding contributions to multilateral agencies

An option for Ireland is a more selective and targeted approach to increasing voluntary contributions to multilateral agencies which reinforce Irish Aid's policy objectives, in particular its poverty reduction focus. As in its priority countries, Ireland might benefit from it becoming less of a marginal player in some of the important multilateral agencies it supports.

There would now appear to be a strong case for Ireland to join the African Development Bank (AfDB) and this is under consideration. The budget is available and most analyses confirm that the Bank's reforms and programme directions merit support. Membership would be another means for Ireland to maintain and enhance the focussed nature of its programme and to bring its experience from working in some of the poorest countries in Africa to discussions at the Bank. Joining the AfDB would also have the indirect benefit of opening up to Irish firms the possibility of tendering for AfDB projects and procurement.

CHAPTER 2

POLICY BASIS FOR IRELAND'S AID PROGRAMME

Ireland's development co-operation policies are based on four documents published during the 1990s.

Irish Aid: Consolidation and Growth -- A Strategy Plan

Irish Aid: Consolidation and Growth described the purpose of aid as providing a foundation on which programmes of sustainable development can be built. The premise underpinning Ireland's aid programme, as presented in *Irish Aid: Consolidation and Growth*, is that the full participation and active involvement of local populations and administrations are vital for development. Without the support of recipients, no aid programme can be successful. Human and institutional development must be integral components of all aid programmes. In order for developing countries to make a significant contribution towards meeting their own needs, support is also required for policies which will allow developing countries to grow, in particular by improving their access to markets and enabling them to participate more actively in international fora where trade issues are debated. *Irish Aid: Consolidation and Growth* described five basic principles which determine Irish Aid's approach to both bilateral and multilateral assistance: need; self-reliance; partnership; gender and environment; and providing grants rather than loans.

Challenges and Opportunities Abroad: White Paper on Foreign Policy

Challenges and Opportunities Abroad[2] positioned Ireland's relations with developing countries as an integral part of foreign relations. Irish Aid and development co-operation is seen as a practical expression of Ireland's foreign policy commitment to peace and justice in the world.

Challenges and Opportunities Abroad presented four objectives for Ireland's development co-operation:

- Reduce poverty and promote sustainable development in some of the poorest countries in the world.

- Assist in establishing and maintaining peace in developing countries by fostering democracy, respect for human rights, gender and social equity and protection of the environment.

- Respond promptly to emergencies and humanitarian disasters, both natural and human-induced, as they occur, and support preventive measures so that such emergencies may, so far as possible, be avoided.

---

2.   Available on the Department of Foreign Affairs' Internet site (*http://www.irlgov.ie/iveagh/*).

- Contribute to building civil society and social solidarity.

While confirming that the main features, aims and objectives of Ireland's bilateral programme were described in detail in *Irish Aid: Consolidation and Growth*, the White Paper specified seven areas on which the bilateral programme would focus: poverty reduction, self-reliant development, partnership, sustainability, human resources and technical co-operation, gender and food security.

Pursuing Ireland's External Interests: Strategy Statement of the Department of Foreign Affairs

Pursuing Ireland's External Interests was prepared in the context of the Irish government's Strategic Management Initiative (SMI) which seeks to reinvigorate the management and performance of the Irish public service. It presented a mission statement for the Department of Foreign Affairs and described its principal responsibilities, primary and specific objectives, and the strategies to be deployed for their achievement.

A primary objective for the Department of Foreign Affairs was given as "to manage Ireland's expanding development aid programme, Irish Aid, and so assist the sustainable development of the poorest countries in the world". It presented the following six policy aims for Ireland's development co-operation (and stated three specific objectives for the programme and listed the strategies to adopt to achieve them):

- Give effect to Ireland's commitment to contribute to the development needs of poor countries, in partnership with the governments and people of those countries and in line with their priorities.

- Support a process of self-reliant, sustainable, poverty-reducing and equitable growth and development, in particular in the least-developed countries.

- Advance the concept of sustainable development in all its aspects.

- Ensure rapid and effective response to humanitarian emergencies.

- Maintain coherence in all aspects of Ireland's relations with developing countries.

- Promote active participation by Ireland in multilateral institutions concerned with development.

Promoting Ireland's Interests: Strategy Statement of the Department of Foreign Affairs, 1998-2000

Promoting Ireland's Interests[3] sets out the primary goals and objectives to guide the Department of Foreign Affairs' activities during the period 1998 to 2000. It was the first of what will become a regular series of strategy statements to be published in accordance with the requirements of Ireland's *Public Service Management Act (1997)*.

Promoting Ireland's Interests presents a revised mission statement for the department and lists seven broad goals derived from this statement. One of the department's goals is to "manage the government's expanding development aid programme, Irish Aid, which is a central component of Irish

---

3.   Available on the Department of Foreign Affairs' Internet site (*http://www.irlgov.ie/iveagh/*).

foreign policy, and work with the people of the least-developed countries, and within the international community, to eradicate poverty and promote sustainable development". *Promoting Ireland's Interests* states that Irish Aid's mission is to "work towards the overall goals of international peace, security and a just and stable global economic system". It presents eight objectives for development co-operation (and the actions to be taken to achieve them):

- Translate the government's development co-operation policy into viable operational strategies.

- Support a process of self-reliant, sustainable, poverty-reducing and equitable growth and development, in particular in the least-developed countries.

- Assist in establishing and maintaining peace and stability in developing countries by fostering democracy, respect for human rights, gender and social equality and protection of the environment.

- Maintain an active diplomatic engagement with relevant countries and institutions, so as to maximise the effectiveness and coherence of development policy and practice.

- Work to prevent emergencies; respond quickly and effectively when they occur.

- Assess and reformulate policy and operational strategies as necessary.

- Strengthen the management of Irish Aid.

- Contribute to enhanced appreciation by the public of issues affecting poor countries.

Consolidating Ireland's development policy and steering growth in the programme

The policy basis for Irish Aid is contained in the four documents described above. While each fulfils a specific purpose, there are overlapping and complementary missions, goals, objectives, strategies, principles and actions. A succinct consolidated statement summarising the main thrust of Irish Aid's policies could promote better understanding of the programme's objectives.

Irish Aid: Consolidation and Growth provided excellent guidance for how the aid programme should expand during the period 1993 to 1997. This was backed by the strong political commitment contained in the *Programme for a Partnership Government*. To steer growth in the programme up to 2002 and beyond, Ireland could usefully consider producing a written implementation programme by up-dating *Irish Aid: Consolidation and Growth*, spelling out how further expansion in Irish Aid will be achieved.

CHAPTER 3

MANAGING IRELAND'S EXPANDING AID PROGRAMME

Role, structure and activities of the various delivery channels for Ireland's Aid

The minister in charge of the Irish aid programme is the Minister of State at the Department of Foreign Affairs with special responsibility for Overseas Development Assistance and Human Rights. Two major and three smaller organisations, all under the responsibility of the Minister for Foreign Affairs, are associated with the delivery of Ireland's ODA. Eight other government departments are also involved in Ireland's aid programme, especially through their contributions to relevant multilateral institutions.

Legislative and civil society input into the programme is provided by the *Oireachtas* (Parliamentary) Joint Committee on Foreign Affairs and its Sub-Committee on Development Co-operation, and the Irish Aid Advisory Committee (IAAC). These institutions are discussed in Chapter 5.

Development Co-operation Division, Department of Foreign Affairs

The Development Co-operation Division of the Department of Foreign Affairs plays the central role in Ireland's development co-operation. It assists the Minister of State in managing the aid programme at the political level and provides support to the Minister for Foreign Affairs in relation to the other aid organisations within the foreign affairs ministerial portfolio. It is responsible for Ireland's overall aid policy and has a co-ordinating role in relation to ODA contributions by other departments. It administers around three-quarters of Ireland's ODA.

The Development Co-operation Division is one of eight divisions within the Department of Foreign Affairs (see Chart 1) and is divided into three sections and a unit for evaluation and audit (see Chart 2). The division manages six priority country programmes, projects in "other bilateral" countries and the NGO schemes and special funds. The division's primary responsibilities in relation to multilateral assistance are the EU development programmes and voluntary contributions to UN development and relief agencies and funds. The division also carries out liaison functions with associated bodies under the responsibility of the Minister for Foreign Affairs -- APSO, the National Committee for Development Education (NCDE), the Refugee Agency and the Irish Council for Overseas Students -- as well as the *Oireachtas* (Parliamentary) Joint Committee on Foreign Affairs and IAAC.

Management and implementation of Irish Aid's priority country programmes are, to a large extent, delegated to the Embassy of Ireland located in each country.

Chart 1. **Department of Foreign Affairs**

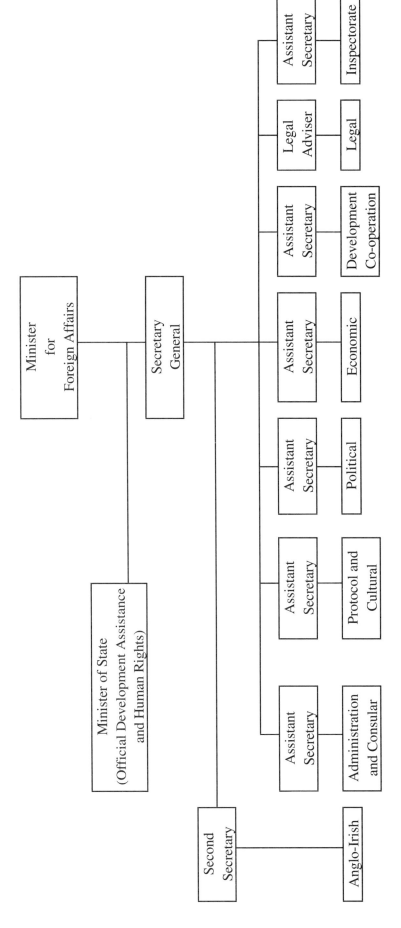

Source: Department of Foreign Affairs.

Chart 2. **Development Co-operation Division**

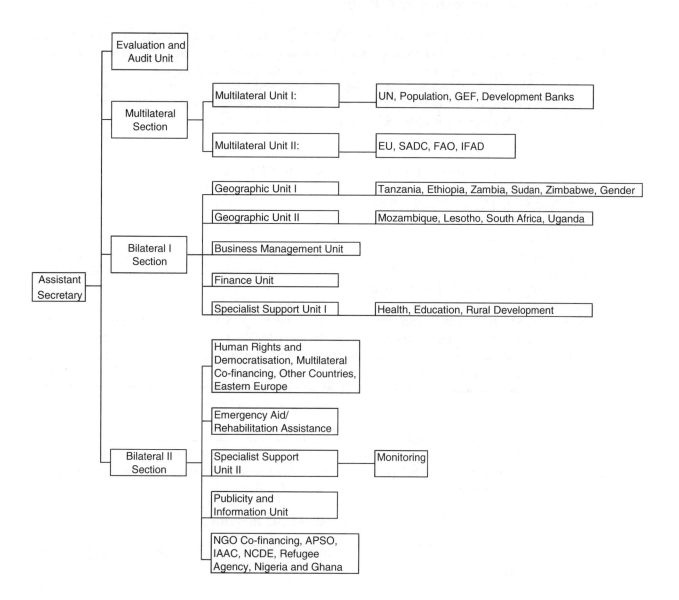

Source: Department of Foreign Affairs.

Agency for Personal Service Overseas (APSO)

The mission of the Agency for Personal Service Overseas is to contribute to sustainable improvement in the living conditions of poor communities in developing countries by enhancing human resources, skills and local capacities in the interests of development, peace and justice. APSO pursues its mission by enabling skilled people from Ireland and developing countries to transfer and share their skills and knowledge, on a volunteer basis, and by supporting organisations and communities in developing countries to work towards self-reliance and sustainability.

The Agency was incorporated in 1974 as "a company limited by guarantee and not having a share capital". Funding comes from an annual grant from the "International Co-operation" budget vote administered by the Department of Foreign Affairs. APSO is governed by an eleven-member Board of Directors appointed by the Minister for Foreign Affairs, including an official from the Development Co-operation Division. Although described as an integral part of Irish Aid, APSO operates autonomously and its activities are administered separately from the rest of the aid programme, both in Dublin and in the field. APSO's strategic plan for 1999-2003 presents six values to guide the Agency's programmes and funding support. These values are consistent with, but different from, those of the rest of the Irish Aid programme.

The Agency funds both short- and long-term assignments and co-funds volunteers with other institutions, mainly NGOs. The Agency provides training for development workers, runs a resource centre and maintains a rapid response register from which people can be deployed for service in emergency situations. APSO participates in the European Volunteer Programme (EVP), is the Irish agent for the United Nations Volunteer (UNV) programme and works with a number of other UN agencies.

In 1998, APSO funded 1 261 development workers in 84 countries (see Table 1) from its grant of $15.2 million. The main sectors of intervention were administration (40 per cent of all assignments), education (26 per cent) and health (17 per cent). APSO's largest programmes in 1997 were in Kenya ($1.2 million), Zimbabwe ($1.0 million) and Uganda ($1.0 million).

Table 1. **Overview of APSO activities**

	1992	1993	1994	1995	1996	1997	1998
Number of volunteer assignments							
Recruited by APSO	..	..	449	470	597	684	630
Recruited by other agencies	..	..	694	796	799	709	631
TOTAL	**440**	**690**	**1 143**	**1 266**	**1 396**	**1 393**	**1 261**
Number of countries where assignees placed	..	..	60	76	86	86	84
Funding for APSO							
Ir£ million	2.5	4.5	7.0	8.5	10.5	10.6	10.7
Constant 1997 $ million	4.2	7.2	11.1	13.4	16.3	16.1	15.6

Source: APSO, OECD.

Half of APSO's assignees in 1998 were recruited directly by the Agency. APSO's own programme activities were divided between long-term development assignments (83 per cent of APSO's direct assignments), the provision of election monitors and supervisors (10 per cent) and a short-term programme for specialists (7 per cent). APSO's co-funding arrangements mean that the Agency supports a wide geographical spread. However, in its own programme, APSO maintains a more narrow geographical focus concentrated on 16 priority countries -- mostly least-developed countries -- which received more than half of APSO's assignees in 1997:

- **East Africa:** Kenya (20 APSO assignees in 1997), Tanzania (21) and Uganda (31).

- **Central Africa:** Malawi (11 assignees), Zambia (16) and Zimbabwe (54).

- **Southern Africa:** Lesotho (34 assignees), Namibia (33) and South Africa (21).

- **West Africa:** Burkina Faso (18 assignees), Gambia (45) and Senegal (5).

- **Central America:** Honduras (6 assignees), Nicaragua (11) and El Salvador (27).

- **South-East Asia:** Cambodia (27 assignees).

One of the initiatives in the Irish government's 1993 *Programme for a Partnership Government* was the mandate it gave APSO to widen the scope of its activities and to increase the number of Irish people working in developing countries. A study was undertaken to determine how Ireland could contribute more personnel and expertise to developing countries. The main conclusions of the study were:

- To meet the target of 2 000 people overseas by 1997, APSO should extend its geographic coverage and its type of placements.

- APSO should spread its regional focus, especially in Asia and Latin America, and should consider extending into some Eastern European countries and some middle-income developing countries.

- Health and education will continue to have a prominent place among APSO's main skill areas but should be complemented by new areas such as public administration, business, technical skills and logistics.

- APSO should expand its existing partners -- Irish NGOs, missionary organisations and international agencies -- as well as develop relations with other international institutions and governments.

Since 1993, the APSO programme has expanded rapidly and most of the study's recommendations have been implemented, even if the Agency has not yet attained the quantitative target set for 1997. An expanding economy with improved employment prospects in Ireland has made it more difficult for APSO to recruit suitable development workers to send overseas. As a partial response, APSO has been shifting its emphasis towards greater use of nationals from developing countries, and has changed its regulations to make this possible.

Irish Council for Overseas Students

The Irish Council for Overseas Students assists with the administration of Irish Aid's Fellowship Programme of scholarships for people from developing countries to undertake tertiary studies, usually in Ireland. The Council provides a range of support services for fellowship award holders.

The administrative costs of the Council are met by an annual grant from the "International Co-operation" budget vote administered by the Department of Foreign Affairs. In 1997, this grant amounted to $0.3 million. Representatives from the Development Co-operation Division and APSO serve on the Council.

National Committee for Development Education (NCDE)

The NCDE is a consultative body established in 1994. Its aim is to encourage and support groups and structures in promoting development education in all sectors of Irish society. NCDE acts as a conduit for government support to NGOs, schools, community groups, teachers and other institutions with an involvement in education or learning. It provides educational advice, resources and support for programme planning, design and implementation. The NCDE's role also includes policy formulation, research, consultation, evaluation and advocacy to promote good practices.

The NCDE consists of 17 members, appointed by the Minister for Foreign Affairs, who represent governmental and non-governmental organisations in the fields of development, education or development education. An official from the Development Co-operation Division is a member of the Committee. A number of individuals with particular expertise or relevant experience also serve on the Committee. Funding comes from an annual grant from the "International Co-operation" budget vote administered by the Department of Foreign Affairs.

The NCDE's grant from Irish Aid has been about Ir£1 million (approximately $1.5 million) each year since 1996. The Committee disburses around three-quarters of its grant. The NCDE receives about 130 applications for funding each year. In 1997, it funded over 80 organisations and individuals, with the non-formal education sector receiving 53 per cent of total allocations and the formal education sector 39 per cent of allocations. These grants were used to produce development education resources and materials; conduct campaigns, courses and seminars; produce drama and audio features; work with schools and students; provide training and in-service development for teachers; and engage in a range of other activities designed to get people to think about and act upon development issues. The NCDE also runs a resources centre and uses some of its funding pro-actively to stimulate new initiatives.

Refugee Agency

The role of the Refugee Agency is to co-ordinate the admission, reception and resettlement of programme refugees in Ireland. The Agency also supports refugees who are able to and wish, on a voluntary basis, to be repatriated to their home country. To date, over 600 Vietnamese and 800 Bosnians have been admitted to Ireland as programme refugees.

The Agency was established in 1991 as a non-statutory body under the aegis of the Department of Foreign Affairs. Funding comes from an annual grant from the "International Co-operation" budget vote administered by the Department of Foreign Affairs but is not included in Ireland's ODA. Ireland does, however, record in its ODA the travel costs to Ireland for refugees, as permitted by the DAC's

Statistical Reporting Directives. In 1997, Irish Aid's grant amounted to $0.5 million. The Agency is governed by a Board, appointed by the Minister for Foreign Affairs, comprising representatives from seven government departments involved with refugee issues, including the Development Co-operation Division. In addition, six observers are appointed to represent the United Nations High Commissioner for Refugees (UNHCR), voluntary organisations and individuals active in the field of refugee welfare.

Other departments

Eight other government departments are involved in Ireland's national effort in support of development co-operation:

- The **Department of Finance** has primary responsibility for Ireland's relations with the World Bank group, including the International Development Association (IDA), and the EBRD, and for the payment of contributions to international financial institutions. The department provides Ireland's advisor to the World Bank and its alternative executive director to the International Monetary Fund (IMF).

- The **Department of Agriculture and Food** provides contributions to international organisations working to improve food security: the World Food Programme (WFP), the Food and Agriculture Organization (FAO) and the International Fund for Agricultural Development (IFAD).

- The **Department of Health and Children** provides Ireland's contributions to the World Health Organization (WHO) and UN population and development programmes.

- The **Department of Education and Science** pays Ireland's contribution to the UN Educational, Scientific and Cultural Organization (UNESCO).

- The **Department of Enterprise, Trade and Employment** pursues policy issues related to Ireland's concerns about the integration of developing countries into the global economy in appropriate international fora, such as the EU and the World Trade Organization (WTO). The department also provides Ireland's contribution to the World Intellectual Property Organization (WIPO) and the International Labour Organization (ILO).

- The **Department of Environment and Local Government** provides funding for the Global Environment Fund (GEF) and the UN Environment Programme (UNEP).

- The **Department of Defence** pays a contribution to the International Committee of the Red Cross (ICRC).

- The **Department of Public Enterprise** provides Ireland's contributions to the International Atomic Energy Agency (IAEA), the International Telecommunications Union (ITU), the Universal Postal Union (UPU) and the World Meteorological Organization (WMO).

These departments work in close association with the Department of Foreign Affairs which, on occasion, supplements Ireland's mandatory contributions with voluntary payments from its own budget allocation.

Internal co-ordination and coherence of national policies towards developing countries

Partly due to the relatively small size of Ireland's government and aid programme, informal co-ordination between departments can still work effectively, enabling Ireland to achieve a good degree of coherence in most of its policies towards developing countries. Discussions occur frequently and easily on a broad range of issues and these views are then fed back into deliberations within the Department of Foreign Affairs itself. Such an open and collaborative spirit is not always apparent in many administrations, even smaller ones. The challenge for Ireland, as the programme continues to grow and inevitably becomes more formalised, will be to ensure that internal co-ordination continues to operate as effectively as at present.

An objective announced in *Promoting Ireland's Interests* is to strengthen the management of Irish Aid by increasing the coherence and synergies between the various organisations involved in the delivery of Irish Aid. Mechanisms exist within the Irish Aid system for collaboration on the implementation of bilateral and multilateral programmes, while co-ordination with other agencies and channels remains more informal. An Inter-Departmental Committee (IDC) on Development Co-operation exists which each year decides on the sub-division of Irish Aid's budget allocation among its various programme activities. This committee comprises representatives from the Departments of Foreign Affairs; Finance; Agriculture and Food; Health and Children; Education and Science; and Enterprise, Trade and Employment, as well as APSO. Approval of individual aid allocations for projects and programmes administered by the Department of Foreign Affairs is considered by the Projects Appraisals and Evaluation Group (PAEG), a sub-committee of the IDC with a more restricted membership. There is also a degree of cross-representation at the level of the various boards or committees that each organisation within the foreign affairs ministerial portfolio has established to set general orientations.

It appears that better coherence and synergy across the 13 departments, agencies, committees and councils involved with Ireland's aid programme is possible. Integration of APSO with the main programme managed by the Development Co-operation Division is one option which could be explored -- as a minimum, closer co-ordination between APSO and the Department of Foreign Affairs is needed, especially in Lesotho, Tanzania, Uganda and Zambia which are priority countries for both programmes. Rationalisation of some of these bodies is also a possibility. Another option would be to expand the mandate of the IDC to co-ordinate the Irish government's various measures relating to developing countries and ensure overall policy coherence. The role of the PAEG could also be expanded to become the project and programme approval body for all of Ireland's aid activities.

As a large exporter of agriculture products and an EU Member State, Ireland almost unavoidably has found its development co-operation objectives diluted at times by trade practices. Subsidised agricultural exports have flooded markets in developing countries which reduces the incomes of local smallholder producers or traditional exporters to these markets and, in turn, impairs the role of agriculture as an engine for economic growth. Examples include Irish beef exports to western Sahel and South Africa and butter exports to South Africa. Ireland is aware that these practices, which represent only a very small share of its export volume, can damage local markets in developing countries. The inconsistencies between Ireland's trade and development co-operation policies have been acknowledged by the Minister of State responsible for development co-operation. Ireland's efforts to avoid such occurrences include an advocacy role for development issues within the Department of Agriculture and Food. Ireland also pursues these matters through its participation in relevant EU fora.

In 1999 as Ireland celebrates the 25th anniversary of its official aid programme, a special statement of national commitment to promoting development and reducing poverty in developing countries as priority goals for all government policy could strengthen awareness of what has been achieved and help consolidate public and political support for further challenges.

How best to manage growth in the aid programme

Managing growth in aid volume

Many DAC Members have seen their aid programmes grow, or decline, rapidly. One lesson that can be drawn from these experiences is that growth which is too rapid or too erratic is destabilising for the long-term efforts of an aid agency and can jeopardise aid quality and effectiveness, and thus the value of the aid programme. Managing a sustained and significant increase in aid well requires setting an orderly growth path, with a clear target, and milestones along the way.

The Minister of Finance's commitment to increase allocations for the Department of Foreign Affairs' part of the aid programme provides Irish Aid with an orderly growth path for 2000 and 2001. However, it is currently not clear how this commitment meshes with the government's target for ODA of 0.45 per cent of GNP by 2002 -- whether additional allocations should be expected in 2000 and 2001 or if the programme will surge from its currently estimated level of 0.37 per cent of GNP in 2001 to 0.45 per cent of GNP in 2002. Clarifying this point and establishing mid-term milestones for Ireland's ODA on the way to the ultimate goal of 0.7 per cent of GNP would be desirable to ensure the programme continues to expand under favourable conditions.

Human resources

To manage Irish Aid's growing programme, the Development Co-operation Division has had to improvise and patch together temporary ways of reinforcing staff capacities, in Dublin and in the field, within complex government staffing regulations. Hiring specialist staff on two-year renewable contracts -- whose role, somewhat paradoxically, is to provide continuity in the programme -- has become common practice. But even with these additional resources, the number of staff currently available to manage the Irish Aid programme -- 82 people in 1999 (see Table 2) -- is widely seen as inadequate and must be reinforced if Ireland's contribution to development co-operation is to be maintained and further enhanced.

To aggravate this problem of resources, constraints on staff mobility and administrative obstacles limit the division's capacity to manage and deploy its staff optimally and to offer career possibilities for all its staff. The division and embassies in priority countries are managed by career diplomats, on rotations of two-to-four years' duration. In Dublin, these people are supported by general service staff, mainly in administrative and support positions, and specialists on two-year renewable contracts. Neither of these latter groups can serve overseas. In priority countries, the programmes are administered by programme officers, on two-year renewable contracts for up to a maximum of five years in any one country, who cannot be redeployed to Dublin. In Irish Aid's structure, only diplomatic staff at the first secretary level can serve both in Dublin and in the field. The Irish Aid system is thus fragile and vulnerable, as within just a few years many, and potentially all, of Irish Aid's current staff will have moved on or been redeployed to another part of the department. Institutional memory and operational expertise will be lost in this process.

Table 2. **Staff levels for the Development Co-operation Division and Irish Aid field offices in priority countries**

	1992	1993	1994	1995	1996	1997	1998	1999
In Dublin								
Diplomats	10	10	11	11	11	14	14	15
General Service staff	14	19	25	33	39	37	37	36
Contract staff	3	4	4	4	7	8	10	10
Sub-total	*27*	*33*	*40*	*48*	*57*	*59*	*61*	*61*
In the field:								
Diplomats	2	2	4	4	4	5	5	5
General Service staff	1	1	1	1	1	1	1	1
Contract staff	1	1	6	6	11	11	15	15
Sub-total	*4*	*4*	*11*	*11*	*16*	*17*	*21*	*21*
Total	**31**	**37**	**51**	**59**	**73**	**76**	**82**	**82**
For reference:								
ODA administered by the Department of Foreign Affairs								
Ir£ million	22.9	36.4	49.9	66.1	78.2	92.6	103.9	106.0
Constant 1997 $ million	38.3	58.3	78.9	104.1	121.1	140.2	151.3	..
ODA per staff member								
Constant 1997 $ million	1.2	1.6	1.5	1.8	1.7	1.8	1.8	..

Source: Department of Foreign Affairs, OECD.

If the current organisational structure is maintained, several changes could be considered to improve performance. One suggestion is to structure a development specialisation within the diplomatic stream which could lead to the highest positions within the Department of Foreign Affairs. This would involve ensuring that most levels of diplomatic staff are represented both in Dublin and in the field. Representation in some of the priority countries could be up-graded to full ambassador status or an ambassador with regional responsibilities for development co-operation could be placed in the field. Where ambassadors are stationed in developing countries, they should be supported by junior diplomats, in programme administration roles.

Creating a core-group of competent, specialised contract staff is crucial for Irish Aid. For contract staff, the present two-year duration appears unnecessarily cautious and Irish Aid would improve staff motivation and commitment through longer contracts, particularly for those with proven capacity. More general selection criteria and job descriptions could be used to recruit contract staff, enabling those who so wished to be subsequently redeployed, thus increasing interchange between Dublin and the field.

The situation of programme officers merits particular attention. This position was created when the aid programme began expanding in 1993. Programme officers have come to play a pivotal role in the management of Irish Aid's programmes in the field. Several are now reaching their five-year limit. Current policy would require their contracts not be renewed, if it is not posible to transfer them to another posting, which would be detrimental. It would consequently seem timely to review the basis of their employment. It would also seem beneficial if some of the experience gained by programme officers could be brought back to Dublin.

The Department of Foreign Affairs has commissioned a review of the adequacy of the Development Co-operation Division's existing management resources, structures and processes in respect of the aid policy and programme. The review is expected to consider options and make detailed recommendations concerning the most appropriate management arrangements for the future, within the constraints inherent in the Irish civil service environment. It is critical that this review results in the provision of the additional staff, in Dublin and in the field, which Irish Aid needs.

As a state-sponsored body and not a government department, APSO has greater flexibility in staffing matters and appears to have more adequate resources to manage its share of the Irish Aid programme. In 1998, the Agency employed a staff of 62, in Dublin and in the field, slightly fewer than the Development Co-operation Division's staff level (see Table 3).

Table 3. **Staffing levels in Irish Aid programme**

	1992	**1993**	**1994**	**1995**	**1996**	**1997**	**1998**
Development Co-operation Division							
in Dublin	27	33	40	48	57	59	61
in the field	4	4	11	11	16	17	21
Agency for Personal Service Overseas							
in Dublin	19	19	26	31	32	32	32
in the field	..	..	..	..	..	..	30
Outposted to associated bodies							
Irish Council for Overseas Students	..	..	..	..	..	..	6
Refugee Agency	..	..	..	..	..	..	9
Irish Aid Advisory Committee	n.a.	n.a.	1	1	1.5	1.5	2
National Committee for Development Education	n.a.	n.a.	6	6	6	6	6
TOTAL	..	..	..	..	..	..	**167**

Source: Department of Foreign Affairs.

With a total of 23 people in 1998, staff levels at the four other bodies associated with the Irish Aid programme –– the Irish Council for Overseas Students, the Refugee Agency, IAAC and NCDE –– appear adequate for the tasks required of them, but generous in comparison to the staffing level at the Development Co-operation Division.

Possible organisational options for Ireland's aid programme

For the short- to medium-term, through a period of consolidation, reinforcing the existing organisation by all means described above would seem to be the preferable option.

In the longer-term, planning and assessment can be carried out on other possible options:

- Maintain the improved *status quo* arrangements outlined above.

- Establish an independent implementing agency for the bilateral programme.

- Create a fully-integrated, geographically-based Department of Foreign Affairs.

- Create an administratively-autonomous aid agency or department, possibly integrating APSO (it is doubtful whether Ireland's aid programme has the critical mass which would make this option a viable alternative).

Establishing an independent implementing agency

This option is probably the most appealing from an operational point of view. The Department of Foreign Affairs would maintain overall political responsibility for the programme as a whole, as well as specific responsibility for multilateral assistance, bilateral aid policy and secretariat and liaison functions for associated bodies, such as the Irish Aid Advisory Committee. An implementing agency could be established as an independent state-sponsored body, which would allow greater flexibility in staffing matters while offering staff greater employment stability and improved career prospects.

Creating an integrated Department of Foreign Affairs

Another option might be to "de-compartmentalise" development co-operation within the Department of Foreign Affairs by creating integrated regional/country desks to take responsibility for all aspects of Ireland's bilateral relations: foreign policy, trade and, in the case of relations with developing countries, development co-operation. This has been done in some other DAC Member countries. It would not appear, however, to be a preferable option in view of the size of Ireland's Department of Foreign Affairs and the dilution of aid experience this option would entail.

CHAPTER 4

IMPLEMENTING THE DEVELOPMENT PARTNERSHIP STRATEGY

Starting with the overall strategy framework described above and exemplified in its bilateral programmes, Irish Aid reflects well the development partnership strategy agreed upon by DAC Members in *Shaping the 21st Century Strategy: The Contribution of Development Co-operation*:

- Ireland is expanding its **resources for development co-operation**.

- The programme has a **poverty reduction** focus, concentrating not just on least-developed countries but on poor regions within those countries, in a partnership approach.

- Irish Aid is oriented towards the social sector and, increasingly, towards support for **basic health** and **basic education**, although the focus could be sharpened.

- Efforts are being made to mainstream **gender** concerns throughout the programme.

- **Environmental sustainability** is being more systematically addressed and additional resources have been provided to support bilateral and multilateral activities in the environment area.

- **Human rights and democratisation** activities are integrated into priority country programmes while in other countries specific actions are funded through a special fund.

Moreover, officials in the aid administration have given careful thought as to how Irish Aid, as a relatively small bilateral donor, can best support the process of putting the strategy into operation and have taken a number of initiatives in this direction.

Putting partnerships into practice

A field visit to Uganda in preparation for this review found that the typical area-based programme, prevalent in Irish Aid's priority countries, strongly reflects the partnership approach based on dialogue and mutual agreement. In the District of Kibaale, Irish Aid works through local structures, building local capacity and institutions in support of locally-defined priorities. Initially, Irish Aid may need to participate in the rehabilitation or construction of some facilities. But, taking a flexible approach often pays off, as in Kibaale, by helping to establish a strong development partnership and laying the foundations for subsequent work. At the same time, Ireland works to support the national poverty reduction strategy as well as Ugandan-led work on sector-wide programmes in health and education. Thus, Irish Aid works at the sector level, aiming at more coherence among donors and greater ownership by national authorities in accordance with the partnership strategy.

Irish Aid's characteristic method of operation recognises that partnerships occur in multiple, mutually-supporting layers -- internationally, nationally and locally -- encompassing not just government but civil society as well. Irish Aid seeks to incorporate the following principles into its programmes:

- Strengthening partnerships and improving aid effectiveness, with emphasis on local ownership and in-country co-ordination.

- Increasing capacity to advance toward agreed development goals and measured progress, with emphasis on poverty reduction and improved indicators.

- Mobilising and monitoring resources for development, with emphasis on how ODA can best contribute to overall needs for development finance.

- Bringing together policies affecting developing countries in a coherent, pro-development orientation and carrying forward the liberalisation of aid procurement in a manner that contributes to greater aid effectiveness while preserving fairness.

Irish planners have identified five areas where Irish Aid could best support the partnership strategy based on experience in Africa: 1) by assisting in adapting DAC targets and indicators to reflect individual developing country circumstances; 2) by helping to enhance recipient government-donor co-ordination; 3) by furthering sector-wide approaches (SWAps) to development; 4) by developing clear policies on capacity building and exit strategies; and 5) by promoting debt relief.

Poverty reduction

Poverty reduction is of central importance for Ireland and its commitment is clearly expressed in Irish Aid policy statements. Ireland pursues a strategy aimed at poverty reduction at several levels. In multilateral fora, Ireland seeks to promote policies and practices which will expand trade opportunities for developing countries and so increase their rates of economic growth. Within its priority countries, Irish Aid concentrates on poor rural areas and ensures that its programmes are explicitly poverty focussed and designed in close consultation with the poor, using techniques such as participatory rural appraisals. Irish Aid also endeavours to maximise the poverty reduction impact of its assistance. For example, realising that investment in road infrastructure has only a limited influence on basic needs and poverty reduction in the longer-term, Irish Aid prefers to encourage labour-based methods in road rehabilitation work to ensure that short-term benefits flow through to local communities in the form of wages.

Ireland participates in the DAC Informal Network on Poverty Reduction, which has studied DAC Members' poverty reduction policies and practices. Based on information derived from that work, the peer review mission to Dublin, statistical analysis and the field visit to Uganda, it can be said that Ireland deserves high marks for steering its programme towards poverty reduction. Poverty reduction is a requirement for Ireland's country assistance strategies. Ireland's aid is directed largely to the least-developed countries (77 per cent in 1997, much higher than the DAC average of 26 per cent). Poverty reduction is one of the main aims of Irish Aid's Partnership with NGOs. The 20:20 Initiative, from the 1995 World Summit for Social Development in Copenhagen, calls for 20 per cent of donor and of recipient country resources to be directed to the social sector. In accordance with the 20:20 Initiative, Irish Aid is strongly oriented towards social infrastructure and services (53 per cent in 1996, compared to the DAC average of 32 per cent). While none of these individual points *ipso facto* makes Ireland's programme an effective poverty-oriented one, together they indicate a clear direction.

One unfinished piece of business in Irish Aid's poverty orientation is the articulation of the linkages in its programme with poverty reduction. While preparing such a document provides no guarantee of effective poverty reduction, it is considered by DAC poverty reduction planners as a positive step in helping to prioritise poverty reduction over other objectives and of assuring that some key elements, such as gender analysis, are not overlooked. In principle, Irish Aid is in favour of working out such a conceptualisation of poverty and the Irish Aid Advisory Committee has expressed interest in helping to formulate it.

Social development

Education

A watershed in Irish Aid's approach to education was the study conducted by the IAAC entitled *Irish Aid and Education: A Report to the Minister for Foreign Affairs* (1995)[4]. As outlined in that report, Irish Aid had always accorded a high priority to education but there was a lack of a clear policy. Ireland has three main bilateral channels for educational assistance: a) bilateral projects; b) APSO; and c) NGOs (often for non-formal education). Irish support in the 1980s went largely into higher education, although the share for primary education began to grow in the 1990s. The report recommended that education continue to be a priority sector with emphasis given to basic education, both formal and non-formal, and that gender issues be more strongly addressed in all Irish Aid supported education projects.

Irish Aid views education as part of the broad poverty alleviation strategy, with the main focus on basic education and with major attention given to gender issues. Although in some instances it is considered justified to contribute to human resources in key areas, the aim now is to give less support for higher education than was previously the case. Whether this exception is over-used is a possibility, but the review team was unable to determine to what extent. Irish Aid authorities should be careful and selective about deviating resources from an emphasis on basic education.

A dedicated channel for Ireland's support for higher education is Irish Aid's Fellowship Programme. This provides funding for people from developing countries to undertake training and tertiary studies in Ireland or, where appropriate opportunities exist, in developing countries. The objective of the programme is to ensure that people from developing countries are equipped with the technical and managerial skills needed to support sustainable development in their countries of origin, in particular by taking over the management of projects after Irish assistance has concluded. To ensure that the programme remains closely related to meeting the basic needs of the poor, Irish Aid awards the majority of its scholarships to people from its six priority countries (see Table 4), uses selection criteria consistent with Irish Aid's development objectives and requires students to make a commitment to return home on completion of their training to resume work and put their acquired skills into practice. To sharpen the poverty reduction aspect of the programme, Irish Aid needs to ensure that potentially disadvantaged groups -- including women, ethnic minorities and the disabled -- are well represented among scholarship holders and that maximum use is made of educational facilities within developing countries.

---

4.   Available on the Internet at: *http://oneworld.org/euforic/iaac/edcon.htm*

Table 4. **Fellowship programme**

	1994	**1995**	**1996**	**1997**
Number of students	181	179	191	230
Share of students from Irish Aid's six priority countries (%)	44	51	57	64

Source: Department of Foreign Affairs.

Irish Aid is preparing guidelines on education along with documentation on experiences in various countries. Irish planners assured the review team of their awareness of the importance of education for girls and of addressing gender issues in preparing these guidelines.

Health, HIV/AIDS and reproductive health

The health sector is a priority for Irish Aid in line with Ireland's poverty reduction policy and support for basic needs. Some of the earlier projects of Irish Aid in the health sector in past years reflected a poor understanding of health needs in developing countries. Some were curative, technically oriented projects, not in line with the international consensus of the Alma Ata Conference of 1978 and DAC Conclusions [see, *Strengthening Development Co-operation for Primary Health Care: A DAC Concern* (1989)]. The profiles called for by APSO still seem skewed towards curative medicine (e.g. APSO advertises for health personnel "supporting curative health care services"). Of course, APSO does work in primary health care, too.

Irish Aid has now moved distinctly into the international consensus on health. New guidelines are in preparation and these clearly state that Irish Aid will only support proposals that offer health and social gain in a primary care setting while recognising the importance of secondary and tertiary services. There appear still to be some health sector projects in the portfolio and even some approved recently that would be hard to justify as being within a sustainable primary health care ambit. These appear to be exceptions and as soon as the new guidelines are adopted and recognised by all staff, these kinds of deviations should over time be reduced and eliminated. Therefore, early review and approval of the draft guidelines would be advisable, following which staff sensitisation about the guidelines would be useful to improve the screening of projects in different programmes under the guidance of the health advisor in the Special Support Unit.

In 1996, 16 per cent of Ireland's bilateral ODA was provided for the health sector, which is over three times the DAC average. Work in this sector is also supported by APSO personnel, in NGO projects and in multi-bilateral projects with WHO, UNICEF and the UN AIDS programme. A working group of IAAC was set up to investigate the longer-term consequences of HIV/AIDS and make recommendations which, following a seminar, questionnaires and field work, should be forthcoming before the end of 1999. In the meantime, Irish Aid has supported a number of activities to address HIV/AIDS (e.g. AIDS awareness in Ghana and Uganda).

In the area of reproductive health, Ireland has a great deal to offer developing countries from its national experience. As recently as 1972, the importation and sale of contraceptives was forbidden in Ireland. After Ireland's *Family Planning (Health) Bill* was published in 1978, rapid strides were made in improving reproductive health services in Ireland itself. Public opinion, according to a poll conducted in 1997 by Market and Opinion Research International (MORI) for the United Nations Fund for Population Activities (UNFPA), not only shows strong support for contraceptive services, sex education and reproductive health services in Ireland itself (71 per cent in favour), but for the provision of contraceptive and family planning advice in the developing world (65 per cent in favour).

Therefore, Irish support for UNFPA is welcome and justified. Tapping into Ireland's own relevant experience and capabilities in this field, perhaps through NGOs such as the Irish Family Planning Association (IFPA), should be explored.

Gender equality

Based on the field visit to Uganda and a review of findings, it appears that gender awareness is strong in Irish Aid, which has a policy of mainstreaming gender equality [*Irish Aid Policy on Gender on an Operational Footing -- Summary of Main Principles and Guidelines* (May 1996)]. This policy guidance grew out of experience from a Women-in-Development (WID) policy formulated in 1986, and the earlier *Irish Aid: Consolidation and Growth* which recognised the link between gender equality and sustainable development as "a fundamental principle." *Challenges and Opportunities Abroad* reiterated the importance of this theme. In mainstreaming gender equality, Irish Aid aims to make it an integral part of the project cycle and an integrated dimension of the programme. Some projects may have a particular focus on women or men when necessary to redress inequities.

With respect to staffing, there is a Higher Executive Officer in Bilateral I Section who is the (part-time) focal point for gender in the Development Co-operation Division. In addition to acting as a conduit for sharing experiences and participating in the DAC Working Party on Gender Equality, this officer screens projects and participates in the appraisal process. All project documentation is expected to address gender equality. Three field offices in priority countries retain locally recruited gender equality advisers. A social audit of APSO in 1997 identified the need for a better understanding of women's development and the environment in APSO's work, which suggests that APSO is taking gender awareness seriously. Fifty-six per cent of APSO development workers in 1998 were female.

Environmental sustainability

Pursuing Ireland's External Interests includes the policy aim of "advancing the concept of sustainable development in all its aspects including ... protection of the environment". Given the scale of Ireland's programme, there are normally no large-scale projects (pollution generating industrial projects, large dams or major infrastructure) that would involve a major physical impact on the environment. However, environmental guidelines do call for grading projects, with suggested steps up to full environmental assessment, so as to avoid negative environmental impact.

In the area-based programmes typical of Irish Aid in priority countries, environment-related aspects could be included as a component and, in many cases, have been. An analysis of this was made in *Irish Aid and Agenda 21: The Bilateral Aid Programme Post-Rio* by Nick Chisholm (September 1998). The upshot of this analysis is that bilateral aid has, since 1993, increasingly addressed Agenda 21 relating to issues such as gender, natural resource management, participatory development and adopting partnership approaches. Irish Aid was found not to have a strategic approach to sustainable development in its bilateral programme. Actions in furtherance of the Global Conventions and Forest Principles were relatively limited, although increasing. However, some examples of "best practice" did exist and most bilateral activities were free from negative environmental effects.

Ireland is active on the multilateral side with participation in the GEF, UNEP and the Multilateral Fund under the Montreal Protocol (Ozone Fund). Ireland makes voluntary contributions to UN Trust Funds (Climate Change, the Biodiversity and Desertification Conventions). Ireland works on environmental issues with the United Nations Development Programme (UNDP) and the World Bank. Ireland participates in the United Nations Commission on Sustainable Development (CSD), the Intergovernmental Panel on Forests, follow-up to the 1992 Rio de Janeiro United Nations Conference on Environment and Development (UNCED) and seeks to participate constructively in international dialogue on environmental issues.

Good governance, democracy, human rights and the rule of law

On the policy level, *Pursuing Ireland's External Interests* reiterates Ireland's policy on development co-operation, stated in *Challenges and Opportunities Abroad* and *Irish Aid: Consolidation and Growth*, which is:

> "to advance the concept of sustainable development in all its aspects including material well-being, human rights, fundamental freedoms, gender equality, protection of the environment, support for civil society and democratic structures and processes, as well as mechanisms to prevent, resolve and recover from conflict."

Irish Aid works on these issues through the angle of human rights and democratisation and, more recently, participatory development and good governance. This bundle of issues is both cross-cutting and a sector in its own right. A co-ordinated division of labour exists between the Human Rights Unit of the Department of Foreign Affairs and the Development Co-operation Division. The former co-ordinates Ireland's approach to international human rights issues and covers human rights questions outside priority and partner countries (for instance in Tibet or East Timor, in the EU and UN, Amnesty International) or which use the diplomatic channel. The Development Co-operation Division administers programmes involving financial or technical assistance. The two work closely together and participate in an Inter-Departmental Committee and a Joint Standing Committee, chaired by the head of the Human Rights Unit. This later committee includes participants from civil society, Irish NGOs and human rights experts.

These types of issues have been integrated into Irish Aid priority country programmes for many years. In addition, a fund for Human Rights and Democratisation was created in 1994 which is specifically aimed at the development of democratic processes/institutions and the promotion of human rights in non-priority countries. In 1998, there were 45 projects in 25 countries with a budget of $1.8 million. The budget for 1999 remains the same. These are basically grassroots projects aimed at empowerment of communities and are usually channelled through international organisations or NGOs, or Irish NGOs.

As a matter of policy, Irish Aid incorporates participation, partnership and local ownership in its typical area-based programmes. Capacity building and improved government is a major focus in all of its area-based programmes. Moreover, all projects are screened to avoid negative impact on human rights. Although these types of activities may not be directly poverty-focussed, Irish Aid believes that efficient and effective governance, public accountability, democratic processes, the rule of law and respect for human rights contributes to balanced economic growth and the elimination of absolute poverty.

To consolidate thinking on this subject, Irish Aid, drawing on relevant DAC work, has prepared a Discussion Paper (January 1998) which will lead towards adoption of guidelines in the near future.

Conflict, peace and development and humanitarian aid

Challenges and Opportunities Abroad outlined a policy on humanitarian crises and called for substantial funding to address them. It envisioned the creation of a humanitarian liaison group to co-ordinate Ireland's response. *Challenges and Opportunities Abroad* also addressed the concept of the relief-rehabilitation-development continuum calling for Ireland to provide significant funding for conflict prevention measures (e.g. support for institutions of civil society and in the peaceful and constructive resolution of conflict).

In accordance with *Challenges and Opportunities Abroad*, Ireland has worked on the anti-personnel landmine convention and was among the first signatory states to ratify it. Irish Aid has funded humanitarian mine clearance operations and victim support, a provision Ireland worked to include in the treaty, in a number of countries [Angola, Bosnia, Cambodia, Mozambique and Russia (Chechnya)]. It helped to fund the WHO Plan of Action for Victims of Landmines and contributes to the UN Voluntary Trust Fund for Assistance in Mine Clearing. Much of Irish Aid's programme is directly or indirectly related to conflict prevention (e.g. strengthening the human relations capacity of police in Tanzania).

To contribute to international peace and security, Ireland supports UN peacekeeping operations. Since 1958, over 42 000 members of the Irish defence forces and *Garda Síochána* (police force) have served as UN peacekeepers. In 1996, Ireland had 750 personnel deployed on 11 UN missions. The Irish government is committed to sustaining the overall level of Ireland's contribution to peacekeeping, however, due to the number, size and complexity of peacekeeping operations, Ireland acknowledges that it is necessary to respond selectively to requests for assistance. *Challenges and Opportunities Abroad* presents a list of factors which will influence the government's deliberations, including the appropriateness of the proposed action, how it relates to the priorities of Irish foreign policy and the extent to which the skills and characteristics required relate to Irish capabilities.

Irish Aid's humanitarian assistance, to save and protect lives and sustain livelihoods, is channelled through Irish and international NGOs and international humanitarian organisations (UN agencies and the ICRC). Co-operation and co-ordination with the European Community Humanitarian Office (ECHO) and UN agencies is aimed at improving international responses to emergencies. To address transition from post-crisis situations to long-term development, a post-emergency rehabilitation fund was created in 1997 ($6.1 million). It is managed in Bilateral II Section by the same Unit that manages the Emergency Humanitarian Assistance Fund, which amounted to $9.1 million in 1997. During the period 1995 to 1998, the bulk of these funds went to Bosnia and Rwanda, and the rest for Angola, Bangladesh, Somalia, other countries, mine action, research and information.

Ireland responded rapidly to help ethnic Albanians fleeing Kosovo with a grant of Ir£0.4 million (0.5 million euro) to the UNHCR in April 1999, followed by an additional payment of Ir£2 million (2.5 million euro) to support a range of measures. The primary focus of Irish Aid's humanitarian response was in Albania with funding through *Trócaire*, Goal, Concern and Christian Aid for emergency programmes. Funding also supported food distribution by *Trócaire* in Macedonia and distributions by World Vision in Montenegro. At a regional level, and in response to the urgent requirement for food and medicine, grants were made to the Irish Red Cross, the WFP and UNICEF. In April 1999, Ireland announced that it would offer immediate sanctuary to 1 000 ethnic Albanians forced to flee Kosovo and that Ireland would respond generously should it become necessary to receive further refugees.

CHAPTER 5

PARTICULAR FEATURES OF IRELAND'S AID PROGRAMME

Priority country programmes

Since the beginnings of the Irish bilateral aid programme in 1974, there has been a policy to keep the programme manageable and well-focussed by having a small number of priority countries as primary recipients of aid. Originally these were Lesotho, Sudan, Tanzania and Zambia. Because of the political and human rights situation in Sudan, and in accordance with European Community policy, project aid to Sudan was reduced in the early 1990s and thereafter limited strictly to basic needs and humanitarian assistance. Sudan has effectively ceased to be a priority country.

Ireland sees the concept of priority countries as having many advantages. As Ireland's ODA volume is limited, it makes good sense for it to focus on a number of target countries, and on specific regions within those countries, where Ireland can make a substantial impact. This freedom to concentrate is a considerable advantage for the Irish programme. Concentrating on a small number of countries enhances efficiency, by economising on overheads, and effectiveness, through good knowledge of the priority country.

In 1993, the planned expansion of the ODA programme enabled Ireland to consider extending the number of priority countries. Choosing a partner country is considered a major step implying financial commitment over many years. The threshold for selection is high and equally so for being dropped. The factors to be considered in country selection were: the degree of need; relative stability; capacity to absorb assistance; demand for skills which Ireland can provide; existence of links such as through the work of NGOs and missionaries; and the presence of an Irish community. Ireland has never had colonies and geo-political or commercial considerations have not entered into the choice of priority country programmes. Since Ireland was already active in Africa it was thought desirable to continue there. A study of countries meeting the criteria focussed on Ethiopia, Mozambique and Uganda. The three were least-developed countries, low on the UNDP Human Development Index, undergoing rehabilitation under stable transitional governments at the time and receiving significant international donor support. Fact finding missions to these countries established contacts with the governments, locally-based officials from the international community, Irish and other aid personnel. Based on this work, these countries were chosen to be priority countries.

Irish Aid presently has six priority countries (see Table 5). About half of Ireland's bilateral ODA was channelled through Irish Aid's priority countries in 1997. While not a priority country, South Africa is also a large recipient of Irish development assistance and received nearly 5 per cent of bilateral ODA in 1996-97.

Table 5. **Share of Ireland's ODA in Irish Aid's six priority countries, 1997**

	Expenditure through Irish Aid's priority country programme ($ million)	**Ireland's total net bilateral ODA (includes NGO schemes, APSO, etc.) ($ million)**	**Priority country's total net receipts from all sources ($ million)**	**Ireland's bilateral ODA as a share of total receipts (percentage)**
Ethiopia	13.9	15.9	699	2.3
Lesotho	6.1	7.2	137	5.3
Mozambique	5.9	6.5	1 077	0.6
Tanzania	10.5	12.5	982	1.3
Uganda	8.1	9.8	778	1.3
Zambia	9.4	10.6	571	1.9
Total	**53.9**	**62.5**	**4 245**	**1.5**

Source: OECD.

APSO's 16 priority countries are not entirely congruent with those of Irish Aid, although four of them are. The reason APSO has a different set of priority countries is that the study undertaken in 1993 to assess how the number of APSO development worker assignments could be increased concluded that APSO would need to extend its geographic coverage and types of placement. Therefore, the government decided to spread APSO's regional focus, especially in Asia and Latin America. Yet, it is not clear why APSO does not devote more energy to all of Irish Aid's priority countries, in closer co-ordination with Irish Aid, so that better synergy could be developed between the two organisations.

Area-based programmes

Irish Aid's bilateral spending is largely channelled into area-based programmes (see Table 6). This approach differs from the traditional integrated rural development programmes, that were in vogue a couple of decades ago, in that they are explicitly poverty focussed; are usually limited to a few sectors; adopt a sequential method; and are designed and carried out in a highly participatory manner with locals and in partnership with local government authorities.

In 1996, IAAC published a paper *Area-based Programmes in the Irish Bilateral Aid Programme: Thinking Towards Best Practice*[5] which shows the extent of analysis that has been done about how to make area-based programmes poverty-oriented. For instance, the balance to be struck between meeting basic needs, livelihood security and income-generating activities. The approach resembles a process approach with a high content of participation and flexibility in integrating elements of the programme into official structures (or not doing so), phasing implementation with pilot initiatives and studies, and making a long-term commitment which is still not open-ended. (See Box 1 for a description of an area-based programme visited during the field visit to Uganda.)

---

5.   Available on the Internet at: *http://oneworld.org/euforic/iaac/abp.htm*

Table 6. **Irish Aid's area-based programmes**

	UNDP Human Development Index rating in 1997 (out of 174 countries)	Ireland's assistance to area-based programmes as a share of Irish Aid's priority country programme in 1997 (percentage)	Location of Irish Aid's area-based programmes in 1999
Ethiopia	169	85	Gurage, Sidama and Tigray
Lesotho	134	--	--
Mozambique	166	48	Inhambane and Nissa
Tanzania	150	20	Kilombero, Kilosa, Muhaza and Ulanga
Uganda	160	60	Kibaale, Kiboga and Kumi
Zambia	146	28	Northern Province

Source: Department of Foreign Affairs.

Clearly, there are intricate management demands on the ground for area-based programmes. It is therefore essential that Irish officials in-country be experienced and highly capable, both in working with local populations and in dealing with government officials. Irish Aid's decentralised method of delivering aid, being so dependent on high quality field staff to manage the programme, means that great care must be taken in expanding the programme to ensure that it can be managed and implemented, on the Irish side, at the high level of performance that has characterised the programme in the past.

Partnership with non-governmental organisations (NGOs)

Many Irish NGOs are quite small, sometimes operating entirely on a voluntary basis. However, Ireland's largest NGOs are as large as those in almost any other DAC country. The largest Irish NGO is Concern Worldwide, whose total income in 1997 was $33 million, of which 38 per cent was from public donations and approximately 12 per cent was funding provided by Irish Aid and APSO. *Trócaire*, which was set up by the Bishops of Ireland, and Goal are two other large Irish NGOs.

In Ireland, *Dóchas* is the umbrella organisation for the NGO community. *Dóchas* has 24 members but some of its members are themselves representatives of many smaller NGOs, such as the Irish Missionary Union which represents nearly 60 church-based organisations. *Dóchas* aims to provide a forum for consultation and co-operation between its members as well as, wherever possible, to help them speak with a single voice on development issues. However, as some of Ireland's NGOs are much bigger, better staffed and have more resources and facilities available to them, *Dóchas* does not perform the role that an NGO umbrella organisation may perform in some other DAC countries of being the principal point of contact and liaison between the NGO community and the official aid programme.

Box 1. The Kibaale District Development Programme

The cornerstone of Irish Aid's priority country programme in Uganda is the Kibaale District Development Programme. The programme is a good example of a development partnership in practice and demonstrates Ireland's commitment to reinforcing democratic structures and involving local communities in its area-based programmes. Irish Aid is integrated into the local administration and emphasises capacity building, community participation and a long-term commitment. To make the partnership work, Irish Aid has responded flexibly giving precedence to Kibaale's development priorities and adapting its own policies accordingly. The partnership has benefited from the high degree of local ownership of the development process.

Kibaale was previously isolated and undeveloped, with little access to facilities. Agreement was given in 1991 to separate three counties from the (then) District of Hoima to create the new District of Kibaale. At the time, social services were concentrated in the "parent" District. The Pachwa road, which provides access to Hoima, had been unpassable for about 15 years. Infrastructure was degraded and none of the District's 500 km of feeder roads were maintainable. The 1991 census found that 84 per cent of the population in Kibaale were engaged in subsistence agriculture, only 20 per cent of people had access to clean water, the adult literacy rate was 44 per cent for males and 39 per cent for females and only 55 per cent of school-age children attended school.

After its creation as a separate District, development remained slow in Kibaale. The District had little infrastructure, facilities or equipment and experienced difficulties recruiting and retaining the qualified people needed to develop the District. Two important events occurred in 1995: activities in Phase I of Irish Aid's programme (1994-96) started in April and government functions, powers and the responsibility for service delivery were decentralised to the District in July.

Irish Aid's financial contribution in Kibaale amounts to around one-third of the District's budget (another 15 per cent is provided by the Belgian Survival Fund). Five sectors have been identified as priority needs at all levels within the District and are included in the programme: institutional support and training; education; health; feeder roads; and water and sanitation. Initially, activities concentrated on necessary capital investment and creating an enabling environment for further development and included:

- Establishing or reinforcing District government structures through budget support, a matching grant for the construction of the District Administration Building, construction of staff housing, provision of vehicles and start-up costs for a vehicle pool.

- Enhancing the efficiency and effectiveness of District staff through training.

- Improving health facilities by rehabilitating the District's only hospital in Kagadi.

- Cataloguing sources of water supply and water needs in a District Water Master Plan.

- Improving or opening up access through the District by rehabilitating, with the use of labour-based methods, the main trunk road through the District and the Pachwa road.

The Kibaale programme has included activities not usually associated with Irish Aid. Budget support was approved as a gap-filling measure for five years, to act as an incentive for the District to increase revenue collection and to demonstrate to taxpayers that development results from revenue collection. Rehabilitation of the trunk road was approved as the local people in Kibaale would be the main beneficiaries. Ireland's basic health focus would normally imply a "bottom-up" approach. However, the International Fund for Agricultural Development (IFAD), funded by the Belgium Survival Fund, was already implementing a basic health programme and so rehabilitation of the Kagadi Hospital would complement this. Provision of staff housing was necessary to attract people to work in the District.

Re-oning the Pachwa road and the Kagadi Hospital were landmark events in the District which demonstrated Ireland's commitment and solidified the development partnership. With a better enabling environment, Phase II of the Kibaale programme (1997-99) could place greater emphasis on basic needs and much has been achieved in each of the five components of the programme.

Irish Aid's programme has made a visible and measurable impact on the lives of the quarter million people living in Kibaale. Local government structures are being set up and staffed, and District domestic revenues are growing by 10 per cent each year. Training in participatory rural assessments is resulting in village members identifying, prioritising and solving their own problems. Primary Leaving Examination results are improving: 19 per cent of students received a first or second division pass in 1994 and 1995, rising to 24 per cent in 1996 and 37 per cent in 1997. The Kagadi Hospital is receiving patients from outside Kibaale and is training health workers who will be redeployed throughout the District. The average occupancy rate at the hospital has risen from 15 per cent in 1990 to 75 per cent in 1995 to 130 per cent in 1998. Road rehabilitation has resulted in the creation of new markets and trading centres, a trebling in prices for coffee producers, smallholder farmers investing to boost production and improved access to health and educational facilities. The District is no longer isolated and is now serviced by collective taxis.

The Kibaale programme is also cost effective, mobilising contributions from local communities and sourcing materials locally, preferably from within the District. In the construction of classrooms, local communities supply readily available materials (e.g. sand and stone) and unskilled labour. Local communities are responsible for maintaining classrooms, protected springs and rehabilitated feeder roads. The programme supports the local economy, including through the creation of employment. During rehabilitation of the Pachwa road, 120 men and 80 women were employed and an estimated 60 per cent of their wages were spent locally, typically on tools for farming, clothes, school fees, medical care and transport. Some of these wages are still being recycled through women's micro-credit schemes. Building construction activities have generated jobs for masons, joiners and other workers. The new culvert-casting yard, which supports road rehabilitation activities, has created jobs for two masons and two porters.

The Kibaale programme shows how, in a propitious environment, Irish Aid can make a substantial impact through a carefully-managed programme which responds to the needs of the beneficiary population in a specific region. However, the replicabilty of this in other districts or priority countries cannot be presumed. The programme has benefited from favourable circumstances, such as strong local ownership and starting when functions were decentralised to the District. If Irish Aid continues its programme in Kibaale, its objective should be to sharpen even more its focus on basic needs. At the same time, it should ensure that its phased withdrawal from the District is seen as inevitable. Supporting Kibaale, or any other area, as an "oasis" of development is unsustainable and would undermine local ownership. The District's future is ultimately linked to developments at the national level. For this reason, Irish Aid should ensure that it complements its activities at the district level with appropriate actions to promote a supportive policy environment nationally.

Irish Aid's Partnership with NGOs is defined in procedures, published by the Department of Foreign Affairs in January 1997, which followed a broad review, in 1996, of the NGO Cofinancing Scheme. These new procedures were welcomed by the NGO community. The development criteria for providing resources are based on: reaching the poor; levels of participation with beneficiary involvement; reaching men and women (gender awareness); relevance; efficiency; effectiveness; and sustainability. Projects can usually be in any developing country on the DAC List of Aid Recipients. There are six Irish Aid programmes through which NGOs can receive support:

- **Block Grants Scheme.** These are provided on an annual basis to five large Irish NGOs: Concern [allocation of Ir£1 million (1.3 million euro) for 1999]; *Trócaire*

[Ir£0.75 million (1 million euro)]; Goal [Ir£0.5 million (0.6 million euro)]; Self-Help for Development International [Ir£0.3 million (0.4 million euro)]; and Christian Aid [Ir£0.25 million (0.3 million euro)]. NGOs funded through this scheme have demonstrated a significant track record in development projects and involvement with the Irish Aid programme. NGOs receiving Block Grants are not eligible for funding under the NGO Cofinancing Scheme.

- **NGO Cofinancing Scheme.** Awards are made up to Ir£50 000 (63 500 euro) with 75 per cent of eligible expenditure covered by Irish Aid. These support one-off projects contributing to long-term development. Irish NGOs can be supported for work in developing countries where Ireland has no official representation. Projects concentrate on basic needs -- food, water, education and health or capacity building. Budget allocation for the scheme in 1999 is Ir£3.2 million (4 million euro).

- **In-Country Micro Projects Scheme.** The objective is to support local NGO activity in countries with Irish Embassies. Maximum grants are Ir£20 000 (25 400 euro) to cover up to 75 per cent of eligible expenditures on the project. Budget allocation for the scheme in 1999 is Ir£1.1 million (1.3 million euro).

- **Emergency Humanitarian Assistance Fund.** The objective is emergency relief due to crises with awards rarely above Ir£100 000 (127 000 euro). Budget allocation for the fund in 1999 is Ir£6 million (7.6 million euro).

- **Emergency Preparedness and Post-Emergency Rehabilitation Fund.** The objective is to provide support to countries threatened by, or recovering from, major crises (e.g. war, drought, famine). Projects are not eligible in priority countries (presumed to be stable politically) or South Africa. Budget allocation for the fund in 1999 is Ir£6 million (7.6 million euro).

- **Human Rights and Democratisation Programme.** The objective is to provide assistance for the development of democratic processes and institutions and for the protection of human rights. This scheme does not apply to priority countries or South Africa. Funding may be provided up to Ir£75 000 (95 000 euro) per year, usually for short-term projects (from one year up to a maximum of three years). Budget allocation for the programme in 1999 is Ir£1.3 million (1.6 million euro).

In addition to the foregoing schemes and funds administered by Irish Aid, APSO expends a portion of its grant to fund volunteers through NGOs and the NCDE works in association with NGOs. In total, Ireland channelled $33.6 million, directly or indirectly, to NGOs (including through APSO and NCDE) in 1996 and $28.8 million in 1997, about 29.5 per cent and 24.0 per cent respectively of bilateral aid. By DAC standards, this represents a high portion of support for NGOs.

Sector aid

Irish Aid has shown strong interest in sector-wide approaches. The objective in SWAps or sector aid is to gain greater coherence among donors in support of a recipient country's own sector programmes. In theory, if donors could agree to provide aid for a given sector in a common arrangement for planning, implementing, and accounting for aid, greater efficiency could be gained in management with improved coherence over the traditional project-by-project approach. Moreover, the ownership of the programme would be more clearly with recipient country than has often been the case in the past.

This approach requires adjustments by donors to how they furnish aid and by recipients in reporting on and accounting for aid received. Irish Aid hosted an international meeting on the health sector (November 1997) and met again in June 1998 with Irish staff from priority countries, developing country representatives and other donors to discuss SWAps further. Irish Aid commissioned a study[6] on the financial aspects of SWAps in 1998 and hosted Mozambique's agricultural SWAp meeting in March 1999.

Irish Aid has contributed to sector programmes in education and health in five priority countries (Ethiopia, Mozambique, Tanzania, Uganda and Zambia). While the theory of sector aid is seductive there are potential drawbacks that Irish Aid is considering as it moves forward into this area. In addition to the loss of individual identity of Irish Aid as a donor in such arrangements, there are questions of implementation, monitoring and accountability that loom large. SWAps have yet to be proven generally effective in practice, which means Irish Aid is still in an early phase in this work. But, Irish Aid has demonstrated its openness to working with other donors to test and improve sector-wide approaches.

Debt relief

Ireland has no outstanding official debts from developing countries. Nonetheless, the issue of contributing to the relief of the debt burden of developing countries has been the subject of lively debate in Ireland.

Like other DAC Members, Ireland has acknowledged that, for a number of highly-indebted poor countries, successful development co-operation will also depend upon concerted international action to alleviate an unsustainable debt burden. For many years, Ireland has advocated a multilateral response to the debt problems of developing countries. In September 1998, Ireland announced its willingness to participate in debt relief measures, agreeing to provide a total of Ir£31.5 million (40.0 million euro) over 12 years to assist the most heavily-indebted poor countries. From this package, Ir£17.0 million (21.6 million euro) is being disbursed in 1999, 11 per cent of aid allocations for this year.

Ireland will contribute Ir£11 million (14 million euro) to the HIPC Debt Initiative Trust Fund, managed by the World Bank and the IMF, which provides relief on debt owed to IDA, and Ir£4 million (5.1 million euro) to IMF's Enhanced Structural Adjustment Facility (ESAF) HIPC Trust. In addition, Ir£7 million (8.9 million euro) is being provided to the IMF to provide interest subsidies under the ESAF Trust. Ireland has also made Ir£3.5 million (4.4 million euro) available to Mozambique for the period 1997 to 1999 and Ir£6 million (7.6 million euro) to Tanzania for 1998 to 2000.

Many Irish NGOs have subscribed generally to the principles of Jubilee 2000, an international grassroots NGO movement in favour of debt relief for the poorer developing countries. However, some Irish NGOs have questioned Ireland's participation in debt relief packages, in particular the ESAF HIPC Trust. They suggest that Ireland's scarce resources should be used for poverty reduction and it is not clear that debt relief will further that aim because the resources that poor developing countries liberate from debt relief are not necessarily used for social programmes. In fact, the IMF

---

6.   See Forrester, P. and McLoughlin, B., *Sector Wide Approaches and Financial Accountability* (December 1998) which sets up guidelines for SWAps and accounting requirements in particular.

itself does not believe that unconditional debt relief will promote sustainable development and poverty reduction. Rather, debt relief should be provided in a process which encourages the adoption of appropriate policies by the recipient country aimed at improvement of social expenditures and stimulating private sector-led growth.

The debate and pressure within Ireland to link debt relief to poverty reduction will no doubt continue as Ireland participates in debt relief measures. The Irish Government, for its part, believes it can do more on the poverty issue by participating in the ESAF and HIPC initiatives than by staying outside. Ireland is also looking carefully at current international initiatives aimed at deepening and broadening the scope of the HIPC initiative and speeding up disbursements.

While Ireland's debt relief efforts will contribute to resolving an urgent problem in the short term, they should not be expected to be a continuing growth area for the Irish Aid programme.

Public opinion, information and development education

Development co-operation in Ireland receives broad support, both from the public and across the range of parties represented in parliament. This has underpinned the strong growth in Ireland's ODA volume during the 1990s. Public support is reflected by the consistently high level of financial backing the Irish public give to NGOs and by the lively debates within Ireland on issues related to development co-operation, such as the recent debate on debt relief initiatives.

To promote public support for development co-operation and increase understanding of development issues, the Irish government provides funds for development education activities through the National Committee for Development Education and set up, in 1995, an information unit within Irish Aid itself. The NCDE's budget has been about Ir£1 million (approximately $1.5 million) each year since 1996 while the budget for Irish Aid's information unit in 1999 is Ir£150 000 (190 000 euro), double its 1997 level. A comparative study by the OECD's Development Centre concluded that the Irish government probably spends a higher portion of its ODA budget on development education than any other DAC country[7].

Irish Aid's information unit aims to promote the Irish Aid programme, give the public a sense of ownership of their programme and increase awareness of development issues. The unit has increased the range of Irish Aid publications; prepared leaflets, fact sheets and material for use in schools; and been active in various media projects, including a twelve-part radio series *Worlds Apart*, television documentaries on gender and development (filmed in Tanzania), debt and development, and demining (filmed in Mozambique), and support for the preparation of supplements on development and human rights published in a major national newspaper. To mark the 25th anniversary of the establishment of Ireland's official aid programme, the unit is preparing a week of activities in September 1999.

The distinction between the NCDE's development education activities and promotion of the Irish Aid programme has thus become somewhat blurred. This distinction need not be maintained and NCDE's activities could well be used more in the future as a vehicle for promoting knowledge about Irish Aid.

The European Commission carries out opinion polls on a range of subjects and these *Eurobarometer* surveys sometimes seek information on European's attitudes to aid, both that from the EU as well as from their own national government. Irish Aid relies on these surveys for information about public

---

7. See OECD, Development Centre, *Public Attitudes and International Development Co-operation*, Paris, 1998, page 86.

support. *Eurobarometer* Report No. 46, carried out in late 1996, is the latest survey available which covers attitudes to aid. It found that an estimated 68 per cent of the Irish were in favour of an increase in Ireland's aid while 10 per cent said it should be decreased. Despite development education efforts in Ireland, 22 per cent of those interviewed did not know whether their national aid effort should be increased or decreased, a proportion above the average for EU Member States (18 per cent).

Ireland has not carried out its own opinion poll on attitudes to aid for many years. It would be advisable to monitor opinion more closely as the aid programme continues to expand, since public support for aid cannot be taken for granted. General opinion polls, such as the *Eurobarometer* polls which also cover a wide range of unrelated topics, can be helpful but the Irish authorities may need to supplement these with periodic polls in Ireland. Irish Aid should therefore consider conducting some qualitative surveys of attitudes to aid which would provide them with more detailed and refined information.

Independent monitoring of Ireland's aid programme

Parliamentary Sub-Committee on Development Co-operation

The *Oireachtas* (Parliamentary) Joint Committee on Foreign Affairs has a Sub-Committee on Development Co-operation whose terms of reference are to examine Ireland's relations with developing countries in the field of development co-operation and the government's ODA programme.

The Sub-Committee meets regularly and receives written and oral submissions from the Government, NGOs and expert witnesses. In 1997, for instance, the Sub-Committee considered the HIPC Initiative, the humanitarian situation in Sudan and democratisation in developing countries and countries in transition. It subsequently adopted resolutions calling on the Government or the Ministers concerned to take appropriate measures to deal with these issues.

Irish Aid Advisory Committee (IAAC)

The Irish Aid Advisory Committee, founded in 1993, is an independent committee of voluntary members established by the Minister for Foreign Affairs. In principle, IAAC has two functions: a) to offer policy advice to the Minister for Foreign Affairs and the Minister of State with responsibility for Overseas Development Assistance on the effective delivery and future strategies of Irish Aid; and b) to undertake research on issues of relevance to the Irish Aid programme. In practice, IAAC is rarely called on to provide advice to the ministers and so its activities have tended to centre on its research function. The Committee's 12 members are drawn from a range of backgrounds, including academia, the development community, the public service and the business sector. They serve voluntarily and are appointed to the Committee in a non-representative capacity as independent experts on development.

In co-operation with the Development Co-operation Division, IAAC organises an annual National Forum on some current topics related to development co-operation. Topics in the past have been the White Paper on Foreign Policy (1994); Gender Post-Beijing (1995); Humanitarian Crises (1996); Multilateral Agencies (1997); and NGOs and Capacity-Building (1998). IAAC has also issued a number of publications on various aspects of Irish Aid (education, agriculture, multilateral agencies, non-formal education and the role of NGOs in capacity-building). In 1997, two Committee Members visited Mozambique with the purpose of understanding the nature of Ireland's assistance programme, providing feed-back to IAAC and writing a report of observations and recommendations which could be useful for the Department of Foreign Affairs. Current work includes environmental issues, poverty reduction strategies, capacity building, health, and development and HIV/AIDS.

The review team was favourably impressed by the high quality of much of IAAC's work, in particular its study on *Area-based Programmes in the Irish Bilateral Aid Programme: Thinking Towards Best Practice* (1996, cited above). In 1998, IAAC made a study visit to Nordic Advisory Boards in Denmark, Finland and Sweden and issued a report with recommendations for strengthening its own work.

CHAPTER 6

RELEVANCE, EFFICIENCY, EFFECTIVENESS AND RESULTS

Staffing issues

With an expanding budget and a high turnover of staff, Irish Aid needs to pay particular attention to a number of staffing issues to maintain the high quality of its aid programme. In such a context, it is important that contract staff recruited fit easily into the Irish Aid system and can make a substantial impact quickly. Diplomats and general service staff may not have substantial or recent experience in development co-operation. Therefore, setting up an on-going formal training programme for Irish Aid staff, in the Department of Foreign Affairs as well as in other associated bodies, would be beneficial. To limit staff turnover, maintain institutional memory and better motivate staff, Irish Aid should consider ways to make its incentive systems more competitive, particularly for career diplomats, as well as try to improve career prospects for all categories of personnel within the Development Co-operation Division.

Management systems

To promote good management practices, manuals, procedures and guidelines capturing essential elements of how to operate can be useful. Irish Aid has done this for its partnership with NGOs and its gender policies (see above). A *Standard Operating Procedures Manual* for Irish Aid's Evaluation and Audit Unit was issued in February 1999 (see below). Irish Aid also has succinct, well-adapted guidelines covering its aid management and project identification, approval and implementation procedures.

Ireland is among the more decentralised of DAC Members. Irish Aid's *Priority Countries Programmes Procedures Documentation* describes the relative responsibilities of headquarters and the field and is a model for decentralised aid management. They state that:

> "Embassies take the lead role in relation to overall programme direction and management. They have central responsibility for managing the bilateral partnership between Ireland and the developing country concerned, consistent with Irish Aid's policy of promoting locally owned development."

Embassies are encouraged to be as self-sufficient as possible (e.g. local or regional purchase of goods and consultancy). Embassies are equally responsible for directing the day-to-day implementation of country programmes. Input from Dublin is limited to strategic-level issues. This places a heavy burden on in-country aid management and calls for an experienced, multi-disciplinary manager with a well-qualified staff, which in the Irish Aid context is small in number. At present, the Irish diplomats stationed in priority countries are *Chargé d'affaires* in addition to managing the aid programme. This adds to the staff burden.

Within the Development Co-operation Division, two country Desks have central responsibility for backstopping and co-ordinating each country programme and facilitating good communications between all staff units in Irish Aid. The guidelines for the Desk are exemplary, including the statement:

> "The Desk's overriding objective is to ensure that the determining influence in relation to programme development is the bilateral partnership between Ireland and the country concerned."

The aid management system relies on a country plan and strategy, prepared every 3 to 4 years but updated in an overall annual planning and budget allocation process that calls for a submission of documentation to the Inter-Departmental Committee on Development Co-operation. Annual submissions include an evaluation programme, an audit programme and a management review of issues. Embassies monitor programme and budget implementation and provide headquarters with quarterly reports.

Project approval procedures are outlined in Irish Aid's *Decision-Making Processes Relating to Approval of Projects and Programmes and Selection of Consultants*. New programme or project proposals are submitted to headquarters as short concept papers for review by the Preliminary Appraisal Committee (PAC). After review and consultation with the country Desk and the Specialist Support Unit, Embassies prepare documentation to submit to the Project Appraisal and Evaluation Group (PAEG), whose role is to examine and approve project documents. To make this process run smoothly, a Pre-PAEG Committee makes a preliminary screening of documentation to ensure that it meets criteria.

The Evaluation and Audit Unit plays a major role in the project and programme approval process. A representative from the unit sits on the committees involved to ensure that appropriate evaluations have been consulted and that relevant lessons learnt have been incorporated into project designs.

Instead of evaluations being seen as a one-off activity or a triennial event, greater self-evaluation of activities and a clear focus on results should be encouraged within Irish Aid. Also, when staff turnover is rapid, the immediate and personal value of *ex post* evaluations is diminished as those people most associated with the project evaluated will have moved on. It is important, therefore, for Irish Aid to promote a culture of evaluation whereby operational staff are continuously involved in monitoring performance and conducting self-evaluations of programmes and projects. Paralleling the style in which area-based programmes are designed, participation of civil society can be encouraged to promote further clarification of objectives, improve communications, increase learning by the people themselves involved in area-based programmes and lay the foundations for follow-up actions.

The field visit to Uganda found that Irish Aid could still do more to engender a culture of evaluation and a focus on monitoring and results. While Irish Aid's priority country programme there is clearly producing results, the programme itself could be more results-focussed. Logical frameworks negotiated with beneficiaries have been prepared which specify measurable indicators and means of verification but it is not clear whether regular monitoring occurs. Nor does there appear to be any systematic reporting against objectives for the country programme as a whole.

While pressures on Irish Aid to demonstrate results may not yet be strong, *Pursuing Ireland's External Interests* foresees a need to introduce performance measurement and management systems. Greater need to demonstrate results will no doubt arise as the aid programme expands and generates more interest in Ireland. Irish Aid would do well to become pro-active in managing for performance, by monitoring and reporting results in terms of pre-established objectives, such as the quantitative and qualitative goals of the *Shaping the 21st Century* strategy.

Evaluation

Irish Aid's Evaluation and Audit Unit was reorganised during 1998. It has been separated from the specialist programme support function and now reports directly to the head of the Development Co-operation Division. Evaluations themselves are carried out by consultants with some participation by recipients and Irish Aid staff. The unit operates on the basis of an annual work programme with a total budget of Ir£0.5 million (0.7 million euro) in 1999. Annex I lists the evaluation reports completed by Irish Aid between 1995 and 1998.

Staff from the evaluation unit also participate in joint donor exercises and work with associated Irish Aid bodies, such as APSO which has no dedicated in-house evaluation function. The unit would like to develop its joint evaluation activities further, for example, in relation to the activities of multilateral agencies.

The evaluation unit remains small, despite its recent reinforcement in capacity, and has two analysts and two auditors employed on two-year renewable contracts. Given its limited staff resources, the evaluation unit has adopted an approach based on multi-annual cycles of different types of evaluations. Irish Aid undertook a series of country programme reviews in the mid 1990s. It is currently focusing on complementary cross-country studies at the sectoral level (roads in 1998 and water and sanitation in 1999). The plan is to return to country studies at a later stage, with these studies drawing on both the previous country reviews and the body of sectoral and thematic material currently being assembled.

Reviews and evaluations of Irish Aid's priority country programmes

A major activity for the evaluation unit in recent years has been forward-looking reviews of the programmes in priority counties. These reviews have covered particular Irish Aid priority country programmes, but not the APSO programme or activities funded through the NGO Schemes in those countries. They have looked at the macro-economic situation, political development, government development priorities and the role played by major donors. Their aim has been to determine the overall relevance, impact and shape and balance of the Irish Aid programme. Such reviews were carried out in Lesotho in 1994, in Tanzania and Uganda (see Box 2) in 1996 and in Ethiopia (see Box 3) and Zambia in 1997.

The original intention was to complement country reviews, two or three years later, with a full evaluation of the impact of Ireland's aid. However, like many other donors, Ireland has found its "first generation" of country programme evaluations to have been overly ambitious in scope. Another limitation for Ireland was that its country reviews could not look in detail at individual sectors. The Evaluation and Audit Unit's *Standard Operating Procedures Manual* consequently states that, in order to maximise the potential lesson learning from projects and programmes funded, Irish Aid will concentrate more on thematic evaluations in the future.

The lesson that many donors have learnt from their "first generation" of country programme evaluations is that they need not necessarily be all-embracing and heavy. Many donors are now pursuing more modest country programme assessments which can provide rapid feed back. Irish Aid should consider this approach when it recommences its country evaluations in the future. In the meantime, a clear alternative way forward exists for Ireland, which is to focus evaluations more on area-based programmes.

Box 2.   **Uganda: 1996 Country Programme Review**

Irish Aid conducted a review of its programme in Uganda in 1996 which outlined lessons learnt and drew up a proposed programme framework and three-year action plan for the period 1997 to 1999.

In accordance with DAC *Principles for Aid Evaluation*, recipient authorities and beneficiaries were involved in the review process. The review team included a representative from the Ministry of Finance. Consultants were commissioned to prepare background papers on each component of the programme in Kibaale, with four out of the six consultants hired in Uganda or from the immediate region. Participatory rural appraisals were conducted in two villages to determine if needs identified at village level were compatible with activities chosen by the District authorities. A workshop was held to seek contributions from representatives of each of the 15 sub-counties in the District.

The review endorsed the selection of Kibaale as a needy area worthy of support from Irish Aid. The review noted that the Kibaale programme is regarded in Uganda as one of the better examples of a District Development Programme. It involves close collaboration with District officials and has neither invested massive capital, as witnessed by other donors in small geographic areas, nor has it been delayed due to lengthy consultations with central officials.

The review proposed that Irish Aid's goal in Uganda should be to contribute to a reduction in poverty through support to government structures and direct support for basic needs projects. Based on its finding that support at the district level is the most appropriate activity for a donor with the resources of Irish Aid, the review proposed that Irish Aid consider support for a further two districts. The specific objectives for the programme in 1997-99 should be:

- Enhance the efficiency and effectiveness of District staff through training.

- Provide an allocation of at least 80 per cent of the country budget for rural areas, while also targeting support for basic needs at district level through government structures [with an annual ceiling of Ir£1.3 million (approximately $2 million) per District Development Programme].

- Include support up to 20 per cent for central capacity building projects which contribute to economic growth or sectoral development and will assist the government to sustain basic services.

- Focus on institutional support and training and basic needs services, such as health, education, feeder roads and water and sanitation.

- Ensure that Irish Aid priorities, such as sustainability and poverty orientation, are used as selection criteria for future activities, and that gender and environmental aspects are integrated into project and programme design.

Box 3. Ethiopia: 1997 Country Programme Review

Ireland's aid to Ethiopia has grown quickly since the programme started in 1994. Ethiopia is now Irish Aid's largest bilateral partner. In 1997, nearly 85 per cent of funding from the priority country programme was directed to Irish Aid's three area-based programmes, in Gurage, Sidama and Tigray.

Irish Aid reviewed its priority country programme in Ethiopia in 1997. The objective of the review was to provide a forward-looking assessment of programme balance, content and progress towards achieving satisfactory impacts in terms of the programme's four jointly-chosen development objectives: poverty focus, community participation, gender sensitivity and sustainability. Where useful and appropriate, the sectoral components of each area programme were also assessed for their relevance, effectiveness and efficiency. The review neither attempted to measure impact of the programme (not possible after too short an interval) nor focussed on issues of implementation performance (which is the task of the monitoring component of the management information system).

As regards the **poverty focus** of the programme, the review found that, although effective, the initial emphasis on the provision of social infrastructure for primary education, primary health and water supply did not constitute a well-targeted strategy for alleviating rural poverty since very poor families, even if exempted from user charges, often could not meet the transaction costs of access. It was generally conceded that the core activities needed to alleviate food insecurity and the low incomes of marginalised groups had not yet been designed and put in place.

The attention that had been given to promoting **community participation** was commendable and serves as tangible evidence of Irish Aid's commitment to participatory development. However, participation in decision-making had mostly occurred only at the implementation stage of the project cycle. Beneficiaries had had no input into defining the problem or deciding upon appropriate responses.

In the area of **gender sensitivity**, the area-based programmes appeared to be moving in the right direction, even though meeting the strategic gender needs of women, arising from women's subordination to men and institutionalised discriminatory practices, is not straightforward. There was a risk that specific sectoral interventions would address only the symptoms and not the causes of the wider problem. The review endorsed the empowerment approach which had been adopted.

In relation to programme **sustainability**, the decision by Irish Aid to work closely with local government and to fund and enhance the capacity of officials in multi-sectoral development units embedded in the local planning offices had clearly provided a sound initial foundation. However, the close support that had been given to the public sector should not preclude exploration of different provider systems, such as the private sector, NGOs and other civil society institutions. A more varied and competitive institutional mix may well offer wider choice and higher quality of service.

The review concluded that the area-based programmes had got off to a good start with a very relevant set of development objectives. There had been particularly commendable achievements in the training of local staff in participatory procedures, in establishing women's income-generating schemes and in the construction of social sector physical infrastructure (primary schools, dispensaries and water points). On the other hand, and for reasons not necessarily or mainly linked to Irish Aid, implementation of crop and livestock-based schemes, natural resource conservation, the improvement of women's position in rural society and the employment component of the labour-based road projects had been less impressive. The review found that management reviews and independent evaluations were a strong part of the Irish Aid management ethos. This enabled unforeseen problems to be detected quickly. The review also considered that the programme was likely to prove capable of achieving satisfactory levels of impact by the time of the full evaluation mission, expected two or three years after.

The Irish Aid programme has a central thrust and comparative advantage in its area-based programmes in priority countries. The approach adopted for their evaluation is consequently of prime importance for Irish Aid. The Standard Operating Procedures acknowledge the central place of area-based programmes and emphasise that the evaluation process should be led by the local district authorities themselves. Only when the evaluation capacity within districts is limited will local or overseas expertise be made available to assist with these evaluations. This is a sound approach from the perspective of development partnerships and the building up of local ownership and capacity. However, as area-based programmes are the core and largest component of Ireland's bilateral assistance, this approach may be placing an unreasonable burden on the shoulders of beneficiaries. Irish Aid, itself, should share some of this responsibility. Obviously, beneficiaries should continue to participate to a maximum degree in any full fledged evaluation of area-based programmes.

Irish Aid's area-based programmes will soon have been reviewed as part of country reviews and from various sectoral or thematic perspectives. While viewing area-based programmes from these perspectives may contribute, as the central pillars of Ireland's aid programme area-based programmes merit priority treatment and should also be evaluated in their own right. There would seem to be considerable merit, therefore, in Irish Aid evaluating its dozen area-based programmes on an on-going basis. This would allow decision makers, both on the recipient and donor sides, to learn from and build on these programmes and would give them the clear information they need to steer the best course. Moreover, and as suggested in the 1998 *Review of the DAC Principles for Evaluation of Development Assistance*[8], such reviews can usefully be linked to current and future programmes, and provide opportunities for participating in formulating recommendations and designing future projects and programmes. This is something Irish Aid will need to do as it expands its programmes.

Irish Aid is planning a bench-marking study of the area-based programme in Muheza, Tanzania in 1999 and an evaluation of the Kibaale programme in Uganda in 2000. This emerging focus on complementary evaluations at the level of area-based programmes is a welcome development.

Evaluations of other parts of Ireland's aid programme

Ireland's aid programme actively supports two types of activity which have received some, but perhaps insufficient, critical scrutiny: the APSO volunteer programme and NGO activities. Other donors have begun to look at these areas just as critically as they do their own agency's bilateral programme. Some of the results challenge common beliefs. In one case, a donor's evaluation of its volunteer programme[9] concluded that it was costly and of limited relevance and lead to the programme being abandoned.

Little evaluation material is available on the activities of APSO. However, the Agency did initiate, in 1996, a social accounting process to measure its performance against stated objectives and values by examining its relationship with different groups of stakeholders. Social accounting started in the United Kingdom in the early 1990s as a way of matching the views of stakeholders against performance criteria, rather than financial efficiency. This approach obtains information by polling stakeholders, but does not question the fundamental orientation or *raison d'être* of an organisation. Its aim is to improve performance and therefore it is a complement to thorough evaluation methods. APSO's social accounting process gave an indication of the strong and weak points of the programme

---

8.   Available on the Internet at: *http://www.oecd.org/dac/Evaluation/htm/evalpr.htm*

9.   See: *Evaluation of Finnish Personnel as Volunteers in Development Co-operation*, Report 1995:3, Ministry for Foreign Affairs of Finland.

from a performance point of view. In response, APSO has put increased emphasis on the quality of assignments and its capacity to respond appropriately to the development needs of the communities and organisations with which it works.

Monitoring and evaluation of Irish Aid's NGO Schemes is being reviewed to see how it can be improved. Each year since 1995, a sample of cofinanced projects have been evaluated (see Box 4) and, starting in 1999, one block grant recipient annually will be evaluated and individual projects will be included in annual monitoring programmes. The overall conclusion from Irish Aid's 1997 and 1998 evaluations of samples of cofinanced projects was that the majority of projects were very good. However, other studies of NGO activities have looked more soberly and perhaps more closely at the real impact of NGO development projects. For example, a joint review by DAC Members of the effectiveness of NGOs[10] found that most assessments of the impact of NGO activities had had to rely on qualitative data and judgements since base-line data was inadequate or non-existent. It also found that evaluations had been conducted rapidly and that most evaluations had focussed on recording project outputs, rather than outcomes or broader impacts. The study confirmed the need to be extremely cautious about making generalisations about the impact of NGO activities due to wide variations in performance.

The study recommended that NGOs be encouraged to strengthen their own capacities to evaluate critically what they are doing, at a level of scrutiny approaching that which other parts of the aid programme receive. One improvement NGOs benefiting from Irish Aid's Block Grant Scheme would like to see implemented is firm, multi-annual allocations, rather than the present annual allocations. This desire is reasonable and would provide these NGOs with greater predictability in their planning which should, in turn, have positive repercussions for the management and impact of their long-term development activities. However, this long-term commitment on the part of Irish Aid could carry with it a reasonable expectation of more stringent demands for these NGOs to strengthen their own evaluation capacities so as to be able to demonstrate the effectiveness and sustainability of their programmes, and their poverty reduction impact, just as other parts of the bilateral programme are expected to do.

Dissemination of results

Irish Aid's evaluations are, in principle, available to the public although details of evaluations undertaken are not well known. Starting with 1998, the list of evaluations carried out each year is published in the Irish Aid annual report and the executive summaries of completed evaluations will be available on Irish Aid's Internet site[11], thus enhancing public accountability. Ireland could also usefully contribute to the building up of a knowledge base focussed on the results of development co-operation by submitting the abstracts from its evaluations to the Evaluation Inventory[12] of the DAC Working Party on Aid Evaluation.

---

10. See: *Searching for Impact and Methods: NGO Evaluation Synthesis Study*, Report 1997:2, Ministry of Foreign Affairs of Finland, prepared for the DAC Expert Group on Aid Evaluation.

11. The address of Irish Aid's Internet site is: *http://www.irlgov.ie/iveagh*

12. The Evaluation Inventory of the DAC Working Party on Aid Evaluation is accessible through the Internet at: *http://www.oecd.org/dac/Evaluation/index.htm*

Box 4.   Evaluation of NGO Cofinanced Projects: Synthesis Report, November 1998

Irish Aid's 1998 evaluation of projects cofinanced with NGOs was based on a sample of 84 projects funded in 1994, 1995 or 1996 in Ethiopia, Lesotho, South Africa, Tanzania, Zambia and Zimbabwe. Total Irish Aid funding for these projects was $2.7 million. The evaluation covered 15 per cent of all projects funded between 1994 and 1996 in these six countries but, as the projects selected tended to be larger than average, they accounted for 30 per cent of total funding.

To facilitate the analysis and summarisation of complex information, a scoring system was devised to ensure that a standard approach was taken. Each project was scored on a ten-point scale against eight development criteria. An average of the eight scores was then taken to obtain an overall rating.

The general findings of this evaluation were:

1. A **high level of satisfaction with the design, implementation and performance of most projects** -- 55 per cent scored as very good, 35 per cent as satisfactory and only 10 per cent as marginal or unsatisfactory.

2. **Most projects were targeted on poorer groups and/or basic needs**, in line with the professed poverty orientation of the co-financing programme.

3. The **gender focus was generally good**, addressing practical needs of communities with a commitment to gender equality in most cases and targets for female participation in some cases.

4. **Weakest aspects were effectiveness and efficiency**, with some examples of relatively high cost approaches, delays in execution and limited impact.

5. The **prospects for sustainability were variable** but considered good for almost two-thirds of the projects assessed, because of strong institutions, cost sharing and programme linkages.

6. An **expected negative correlation between poverty focus and sustainability did not emerge**.

7. There was a **broad correlation between ownership and sustainability** but it was not particularly strong; social service projects scored highly on sustainability if they were backed by strong institutions (usually churches) even if communities participated only as consumers of services.

8. **Good projects tended to score well in all respects** while weak projects scored poorly on most counts.

9. There was **little variation in performance across sectors** but the results in water and sanitation were more consistent than in other areas.

10. There were **no significant differences in performance between smaller and larger projects**.

11. **Differences in performance between different types of implementing agencies were small** – local NGOs achieved slightly higher scores while Irish/international NGOs were most consistent.

These findings support the main conclusion of the 1997 evaluation, that the Cofinancing Scheme is achieving its main objective of poverty-oriented development in a cost-effective way in most cases. However, since the analysis did not reveal any consistent patterns of strengths or weaknesses, there are few general lessons for project selection or scheme management arising out of either evaluation.

There has been a clear evolution in Irish Aid's evaluation reports. Formerly, evaluations were written for specific, strictly internal purposes. In general, these evaluations found that Irish Aid projects were almost uniformly successful and probably could have been more incisive in their analysis. The presentation of these reports varied considerably. Some lacked cohesion and were "reader-unfriendly" to the point that it was difficult to determine basic project information (stated project objectives or logical framework; key dates; resources/funding provided, by Ireland and the recipient government; procurement methods; staffing; description of implementation mechanism; interim evaluations; inputs; and, most importantly, impact or results obtained). While some of this information is provided, it was difficult to find and generally not well marshalled. From a comparative standpoint and as regards their analysis and presentation, many of these earlier evaluations do not stand up well along side other DAC Member evaluations the Secretariat has reviewed.

The latest generation of Irish Aid evaluations are written for publication and there has been a noticeable improvement in the format, analysis and presentation of these reports. The 1998 *Study of Irish Aid Road Projects*, which assessed assistance to the road sector in four priority countries, is a good example of the improvements that have been introduced in evaluations.

CHAPTER 7

IRELAND'S ASSISTANCE THROUGH MULTILATERAL AGENCIES

Ireland's development co-operation programme initially consisted almost entirely of mandatory contributions to international organisations, such as the UN development agencies. Following Ireland's accession to the European Community (EC) in 1973, ODA started growing more systematically, through Ireland's contribution to the EC's development programmes and through the establishment of the Department of Foreign Affairs' bilateral assistance programmes. APSO began operating in 1974 and the Department of Foreign Affairs set up three priority country programmes in 1975. The proportion of Ireland's ODA channelled through multilateral agencies has consequently been on a downward path. During the mid 1970s, Ireland's multilateral assistance exceeded 80 per cent of total ODA but by 1992 its share had fallen to 60 per cent.

Irish Aid: Consolidation and Growth recognised that some development tasks are beyond the scope of individual bilateral donors, especially small donors, and that an appropriate balance between bilateral and multilateral assistance is important. At the same time, it noted that Ireland's multilateral share was disproportionately large, by comparison with its EC partners, and that this balance should be redressed as the programme expands. Ireland now directs around one third of its ODA through multilateral agencies.

During consultations to prepare *Challenges and Opportunities Abroad*, it was apparent that there was a widely held view in Ireland that its multilateral contributions were being absorbed into large institutional budgets with limited Irish influence over the policy objectives. Ireland now gives a high priority to monitoring the efficiency and effectiveness of multilateral agencies and to seeking to influence their roles and work. To help achieve this objective, Ireland actively seeks membership on the Executive Boards of multilateral institutions. Ireland also monitors the activities of multilateral agencies in the field through its embassies to ensure that they are performing effectively and using their funds as efficiently as possible and in the best interest of developing countries.

Ireland's immediate objective for its multilateral assistance during the period 1998-2000, as presented in *Promoting Ireland's Interests*, is to work through the EU, the UN and the international financial and trade institutions to develop and implement programmes which enhance the development prospects of poor countries, including through a successor arrangement to the Lomé Convention.

European Union

Reflecting the fact that the EU is a composite of its Member States and not an independent institution, Ireland, as a Member State, has confidence in its ability to influence discussions and committee decisions at the European level. Ireland has consequently tried to become more active in EU committees and works hard to prepare its positions on issues to be debated by EU Member States.

For Ireland, the important challenge for the EU is to strengthen coherence between all of its policies and programmes affecting developing countries as well as increase co-ordination between the EU's development policies and programmes and those of its Member States. For its part, the Department of Foreign Affairs works closely with other departments to formulate coherent positions on such issues as EU trade policy.

Ireland increased its share of contributions to the European Development Fund (EDF) from 0.55 per cent for the 7th EDF (1990-95) to 0.6 per cent for the 8th EDF (1996-2000). During debates on a successor agreement to the Lomé Convention after 2000, Ireland has argued in favour of the needs of least-developed countries, especially in sub-Saharan Africa.

Like several other EU Member States, Ireland would like to see a larger share of EU development assistance going to least-developed countries.

United Nations agencies

Ireland sees the United Nations system as having four distinct advantages: size and capacity; a global network of offices; neutrality; and its aid is not tied. Its co-ordination role in the field, particularly for humanitarian aid, is important.

While recognising the validity of some criticisms about the UN system, Ireland believes the primacy of the UN as a system merits defending. There is, nonetheless, a need for all UN Members to clarify the comparative advantage and specialisation of the various agencies and funds and to ensure that they are operating in a complementary fashion. Ireland consequently endorses the UN's reform and renewal process. During Ireland's Presidency of the European Union in 1996, a common EU position paper on UN economic and social reform was drawn up for consideration by the UN Secretary-General.

Ireland provides voluntary contributions to a number of UN development and relief agencies and funds. *Irish Aid: Consolidation and Growth* described Ireland's contributions to UN agencies as comparatively modest and included the intention to increase contributions steadily as the programme expands, with the UNDP, UNICEF and UNHCR to remain the largest beneficiaries. *Challenges and Opportunities Abroad* included the intention to increase Ireland's voluntary contributions to UN agencies until they are comparable, as a share of GNP, with the average of the other donor countries.

Ireland's voluntary contributions to UN agencies and funds have increased nearly fourfold between 1993 and 1999, from Ir£2.5 million ($3.7 million) to Ir£8.8 million ($11 million). Decisions on the level of contributions to particular agencies have taken account of their progress in implementing reforms.

The UNDP is the largest beneficiary of Ireland's voluntary contributions with 30 per cent of contributions in 1999. Ireland recognises that the UNDP has been through a difficult period and its funding has declined. Ireland approves generally of UNDP policies but finds that at an operational level it is spread too widely and too thinly. The UNDP has reformed itself: by undertaking an internal re-organisation which better promotes partnership with developing countries; by moving towards a results-based approach; and by organising international conferences on key areas related to development.

Ireland also pursues the aim of assisting as many other useful UN programmes as possible. As a result, the number of agencies supported has increased from 13 in 1993 to 39 in 1999. Some of these contributions are symbolic -- 15 agencies or funds received Ir£50 000 (63 500 euro) or less in 1999, with five receiving just Ir£15 000 (19 000 euro). But, importantly for Ireland, these contributions allow it to attend meetings and contribute to and participate in debates.

Ireland's voluntary contributions provide core resources, often unear-marked, and cover the broad range of UN activities: human rights, assistance to refugees, democracy building, electoral reform, education and training, health, humanitarian relief, mine-clearing, environmental protection, trade and enterprise promotion and international action against drugs. Half of Ireland's contribution to the UN Volunteers programme is, however, ear-marked for activities associated with projects to which Irish APSO-sponsored personnel are assigned. Ear-marking of funds also occurs with the WHO and the UN Institute for Training and Research (UNITAR).

In line with Ireland's objective to enhance its monitoring of the effectiveness of UN agencies and influence their work, Ireland was a member of the Executive Boards of UNHCR and WHO until 1997, was a member of the Boards of FAO, UNICEF and UNITAR in 1998, is serving as a member of the Board of UNDP, from 1998 to 2000, and will join the Board of WFP in 2001 and the Board of UNICEF in 2002. Ireland intends to stand for election to the UN Security Council in 2000.

Development banks

Ireland values the commitment of the World Bank to poverty reduction and long-term development in the poorest countries. This was reflected in its decision, in 1998, to provide a substantial voluntary supplementary contribution to the 12th replenishment of IDA. Ireland's pledge of Ir£20 million (about $28 million) amounted to 0.26 per cent of donors' total pledges, significantly more than the 0.18 per cent that Ireland was expected to contribute, based on its GNP, and included a supplementary payment of Ir£5 million (about $7 million).

As discussed in Chapter 5, Ireland has long advocated a lasting resolution to the debt problem of the poorest and most indebted developing countries. Ireland supports the HIPC Initiative and will continue to press for particular emphasis on the social aspects of structural adjustment programmes.

Co-financing with multilateral agencies: multi-bi assistance

Co-financing actions with multilateral agencies enables Ireland to broaden its activities into areas it would not otherwise reach through its bilateral programme. It can also provide an additional and useful source of knowledge and experience from which Ireland can benefit when formulating its own policies and programmes.

Ireland co-finances activities with the International Fund for Agricultural Development; the Economic Development Institute (EDI), the training and human resources development agency of the World Bank; three centres of the Consultative Group on International Agricultural Research (CGIAR) whose research is most relevant to the problems in Irish Aid's priority countries; and the Association for the Development of African Education (ADEA), particularly their work linked to the activities of the EDI.

Ireland has maintained a consultancy trust fund at the World Bank since 1986, used to finance assignments awarded to Irish firms and individuals in a range of sectors. *Irish Aid: Consolidation and Growth* found that it would be desirable to identify ways of increasing the share of contracts awarded to Irish companies by international aid agencies and Ireland has subsequently created two additional trust funds. In 1993, a fund was set up at the EBRD to finance studies and monitoring work carried out Irish consultants and, in 1995, a fund was established at the International Financial Corporation (IFC) of the World Bank to finance consultancy work carried out by Irish firms and to assist private sector development.

CHAPTER 8

BASIC PROFILES

Aid volume

Official development assistance (ODA)

Between 1991-92 and 1996-97, Ireland had the fastest growing ODA programme in the DAC, expanding by an average of 20.1 per cent a year in real terms (see Annex Table II-6). Ireland's net ODA rose steadily from $70 million in 1992 to $187 million in 1997 (see Table II-1).

As a share of national income, Ireland's ODA rose from 0.16 per cent of GNP in 1992 -- the poorest result recorded by a DAC country that year -- to 0.31 per cent of GNP in 1997, the 10th rank in the DAC (see Figure II-3). Ireland's ODA/GNP ratio has exceeded the DAC average each year since 1995 but is still below the DAC average country effort (unweighted average) (see Figure 1). In 1997, Ireland's ODA/GNP performance was seventh amongst EU Member States, but remained below the EU average (0.33 per cent).

Figure 1.   **ODA as a percentage of GNP**

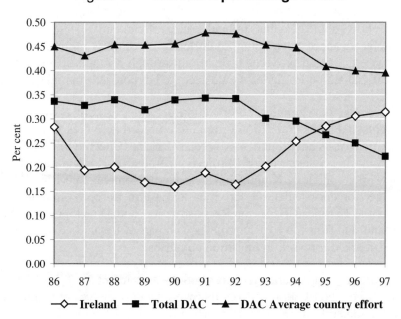

Source: OECD.

In its 1993 *Programme for Partnership Government*, the Irish government pledged to increase Ireland's ODA to 0.20 per cent of GNP in 1993 and by 0.05 per cent of GNP each year thereafter, so as to put Ireland on a par with many of its European partners and make steady progress towards achieving the UN goal of 0.7 per cent of GNP. Based on GNP estimates available in mid 1993, *Irish Aid: Consolidation and Growth* projected the financial resources that would be needed to meet these targets (see Table 7). The target for ODA volume was exceeded in 1994, 1995 and 1996 but was not met in 1997 (although the 1997 target was reached in 1998). Ireland's ODA/GNP ratio was on target in 1993 and 1994 but rapid growth in Ireland's GNP, which increased by 43 per cent in real terms between 1992 and 1997, meant that the ratio quickly started to fall behind target in subsequent years.

Table 7. **Targets set in 1993 for Ireland's ODA**

	1993	1994	1995	1996	1997	1998
Projected performance						
ODA volume (Ir£ million)	-	71	90	110	135	n.a.
ODA/GNP ratio (%)	0.2	0.25	0.30	0.35	0.40	n.a.
Actual performance						
ODA volume (Ir£ million)	54.7	75.2	96.1	112.0	124.1	139.6
ODA/GNP ratio (%)	0.22	0.25	0.29	0.31	0.31	0.30

Source: Department of Foreign Affairs.

In 1998, Ireland's net ODA disbursements were $199 million (Ir£ 140 million), the equivalent of 0.30 per cent of GNP. Budget allocations for aid for 1999 are Ir£178 million (226 million euro), a projected 0.35 per cent of GNP.

Official aid

Data supplied to the DAC indicates that Ireland's net official aid disbursements to countries in transition and the more advanced developing countries fell from $21 million in 1995 to $1 million 1996 and 1997. However, Ireland provides official aid through a range of bilateral and multilateral mechanisms and its official aid performance would seem to be more substantial than reported.

Some of Irish Aid's regular development co-operation activities benefit countries in transition. In 1997, the Human Rights and Democratisation Programme funded activities in Russia (Chechnya), the Emergency Humanitarian Assistance Fund was used in Russia (Chechnya) and the Czech Republic while the NGO Co-Financing Scheme funded projects in Bulgaria, Romania and Russia. APSO has placed development workers in Hong Kong, China; Poland; Romania and Russia (Chechnya). Irish Aid has a small budget for direct bilateral activities in Eastern Europe. Ireland funds a Technical Co-operation Fund at the European Bank for Reconstruction and Development, which finances the work of Irish consultants and firms on EBRD projects, and part of Ireland's Consultancy Trust Fund at the World Bank is ear-marked for work in transition countries.

Ireland's multilateral official aid includes its contributions as a member of the EBRD and a share of the official aid disbursed by the EU funded from its own budget resources credited back on a *pro rata* basis. However, no multilateral official aid was notified for either 1996 or 1997.

ODA composition

Irish Aid: Consolidation and Growth included the intention for expenditure on both bilateral and multilateral assistance to increase substantially, but with bilateral funding to increase at a faster rate than multilateral so as to achieve a situation where two-thirds of aid is bilateral and one third multilateral. Between 1993 and 1997, Ireland's bilateral ODA nearly trebled, in real terms, while multilateral assistance increased by 50 per cent. The share of multilateral assistance in Ireland's programme fell from approximately 60 per cent at the beginning of the 1990s to 35.6 per cent in 1997, close to the average for EU Member States (35.1 per cent) but slightly above the DAC average (33.1 per cent) (see Table II-6 and Figure 2).

As planned in *Irish Aid: Consolidation and Growth*, the expansion in Ireland's bilateral aid programme has principally occurred through increases in technical co-operation, project and programme aid, and emergency and disaster relief (see Table II-2). Current commitments for bilateral debt relief actions, for Mozambique and Tanzania, began in 1997 and will continue until 2000. By DAC standards, Ireland channels a considerable amount of its ODA through various NGO funding schemes -- an estimated 15 per cent of total ODA in 1997 -- but as Ireland does not notify the amounts involved to the DAC, the corresponding figures do not appear in Table II-2. Ireland has no funds or public financial institutions that directly finance export credits and no programme for associated financing.

The major portion of Ireland's multilateral assistance is through the EC, both Ireland's share of the EU's ODA budget resources and contributions to the European Development Fund. Together these accounted for more than one fifth of Ireland's ODA in 1997. Ireland also makes mandatory and voluntary contributions to UN agencies -- particularly the UNDP, UNHCR and UNICEF -- as well as provides support to the World Bank group. Ireland is not a member of any of the regional development banks whose activities primarily favour developing countries (although Ireland is a member of the EBRD). Ireland supports the promotion of food security in developing countries through its contributions to the Food Aid Convention, FAO, WFP and IFAD, as well as through its support for the EU's Food Security and Food Aid budget.

Figure 2.   Share of multilateral ODA in total ODA

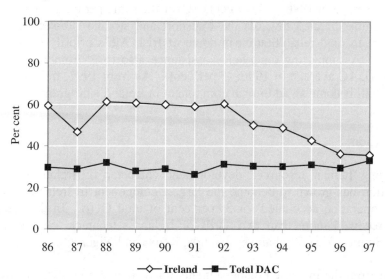

Source: OECD.

79

Geographic distribution of bilateral ODA

With its clear concentration on sub-Saharan Africa and least-developed countries, Ireland's bilateral aid programme is among the most strongly focussed in the DAC. In 1997, Ireland's gross ODA disbursements to sub-Saharan Africa accounted for 86 per cent of its allocable bilateral ODA (DAC average: 30 per cent) whilst assistance to least-developed countries accounted for 77 per cent (DAC average: 26 per cent) (see Table II-3). Irish ODA to least-developed countries, both bilateral and through multilateral agencies, reached 0.15 per cent of GNP for the first time in 1997 (DAC average: 0.05 per cent) (see Table II-6).

Although Ireland's bilateral programme has managed, by DAC standards, to remain focussed as the aid budget has increased, some signs are apparent of a tendency to greater geographic dispersion. In 1986-87, 76 per cent of allocable bilateral gross disbursements were channelled to Irish Aid's four priority countries (see Table II-4). By 1991-92, this share had fallen to 58 per cent and by 1996-97, Irish Aid's six priority countries received 56 per cent of bilateral ODA. Another indication of the growing dispersion in Ireland's programme is the number of recipients: 50 countries in 1986-87, 63 in 1991-92, rising to 105 in 1996-97. Some of the reasons for this greater geographic dispersion are the increase in size and number of Irish Aid's "other bilateral" country programmes and increased financing for programmes which can be disbursed in most developing countries: the various NGO schemes (including the Cofinancing Scheme, funding for which increased fourfold between 1992 and 1997), the new funds for human rights and democratisation and for post-emergency rehabilitation, and the APSO programme.

Sectoral distribution of bilateral ODA

The evolution of the sectoral distribution of Ireland's bilateral assistance shows both a greater concentration on social sectors and growing support for other types of activities. In 1996, more than half of Ireland's bilateral ODA disbursements supported the social infrastructure and services sector, in particular education and, increasingly, health and water supply and sanitation (see Table II-5). Ireland's level of support was significantly more than the DAC average of 32 per cent. The share of Ireland's bilateral ODA directed towards productive sectors fell from 24 per cent in 1986-87 to 7 per cent in 1996 (DAC average in 1996: 14 per cent). Over the same period, a small rise occurred in the share of the programme directed towards the transport and storage sub-sector, reflecting Ireland's growing involvement in road rehabilitation in some of Irish Aid's priority countries. The share of Ireland's bilateral ODA supporting emergency assistance also rose, from 4 per cent in 1986-87 to 16 per cent in 1996 (DAC average in 1996: 5 per cent). As from 1997, Ireland's actions relating to bilateral debt relief will become an additional component in Ireland's programme.

Technical co-operation

Reflecting the strong human resources development character of Ireland's bilateral assistance, technical co-operation has grown to become the largest component in Ireland's aid programme. In 1997, technical co-operation accounted for 39 per cent of total ODA. In that year, Irish Aid's six priority countries received more than two-thirds of Ireland's technical co-operation. Other large beneficiaries were South Africa, Zimbabwe, Rwanda, Kenya and Nigeria.

While not apparent from the increased disbursements for technical co-operation, Ireland has reduced by two-thirds the number of expatriate technical assistants in its priority countries, from 70 in 1992 to

25 in 1998. Over the same period, Ireland has increased its use of local technical experts and trebled, since 1992, the number of APSO development workers in developing countries.

Procurement policies and aid tying

Recognising that the reasons for giving ODA are first and foremost humanitarian, purchases of supplies for Ireland's aid programme are unrestricted and have traditionally not been tied to the purchase of Irish goods. In practice, most supplies are purchased within recipient countries or from international suppliers. Less than 1 per cent of ODA funds purchases from Ireland.

At the same time, several parts of Ireland's aid programme are almost inevitably spent in Ireland. An internal Irish Aid study conducted in 1996 found that expenditures in Ireland could represent close to 30 per cent of the bilateral budget, i.e. nearly $35 million. Technical assistance frequently involves the use of Irish consultants. Many of the costs associated with the training of nationals from developing countries, including through the Fellowship Programme, are spent in Ireland. APSO development workers, almost all of whom are Irish, receive a resettlement grant on their return home. Ireland's consultancy trust funds with the World Bank and EBRD are reserved for Irish consultants and firms. By their nature, NCDE's development education activities and headquarter administrative costs involve expenditures in Ireland.

As regards Ireland's emergency humanitarian assistance, *Irish Aid: Consolidation and Growth* proposed that, while taking account of the needs of individual situations and the cost effectiveness of emergency assistance operations, every effort will be made to ensure that as much as possible of the material, medicine, food products, blankets and equipment provided are Irish made.

In some isolated cases, Ireland also restricts tendering to Irish firms. This occurred in Uganda for the tender to prepare the road design for the trunk road running through the District of Kibaale. Subsequently, when Irish Aid agreed to fund another project to rehabilitate the trunk road leading into the district, the Ugandan government requested that the same Irish firm be used again.

Other financial flows to developing and transition countries

Grants by non-governmental organisations (NGOs)

Support for the development co-operation activities of NGOs is strong in Ireland, reflecting both Ireland's history of direct contact with developing countries through its missionary tradition and a profound sense of solidarity between the Irish and people in developing countries. In 1997, grants by NGOs totalled $56 million, the equivalent of 0.09 per cent of GNP. Ireland's private grants/GNP ratio is the second highest in the DAC, just behind the Netherlands (0.10 per cent) and ahead of Norway (0.08 per cent).

Private flows at market terms

Reporting of Ireland's private flows to developing and transition countries appears incomplete and this hampers a full analysis of Ireland's financial relations. Between 1992 and 1995, Ireland's notifications of private flows consisted of export credits, while for 1996 and 1997 flows were notified for bilateral portfolio investments. It is possible that Ireland's total private flows take a number of different forms each year and are, in total, more substantial than the figures reported to the DAC.

Statistical reporting

Ireland reports to the DAC on two core tables only: DAC 1 on official and private flow aggregates and DAC 2a on the geographical distribution of ODA disbursements. Due to limited resources being available in Dublin for statistical work, no data on ODA commitments or tying status are reported to the DAC and data on sectoral distribution is reported irregularly. Ireland's private sector flows to developing countries are only reported in aggregate on DAC Table 1, no breakdown by recipient country is provided. Ireland does not report on individual commitments to the Creditor Reporting System (CRS).

Some notable improvements are to be expected from Ireland's statistical reporting in the future, as a new computer system is being set up to collect and compile data. This should enable Ireland to report to the CRS and to submit more complete data to the DAC, especially on commitments and the sectoral distribution of ODA.

ANNEX I

EVALUATIONS CONDUCTED BY IRISH AID'S EVALUATION AND AUDIT UNIT, 1995-99

1995 EVALUATIONS

Fellowships programme

Kilosa District Rural Development Programme – Tanzania

NGO Co-Financing Scheme

1996 EVALUATIONS

Country Programme Review - Uganda

Country Programme Review - Zimbabwe

Hotel and Tourism Training Project – Zambia

Labour Construction Unit Review - Lesotho

Lusaka Maternity Clinics Project - Zambia

NGO Co-Financing Scheme

Small Scale Enterprise Developments Projects - Zambia

Women's Training Centres - Bangladesh

1997 EVALUATIONS

Basotho Ponies – Lesotho

BESA – Zimbabwe

Bosnia and Herzegovina Rehabilitation

Capital and Training Project – Zambia

Chilanga Cement – Zambia

Country Programme Review - Ethiopia

Electricity Supply Board International Upgrade in Phnom Penh - Cambodia

Evelyn Hone College – Zambia

Hydrology Project – Tanzania

Irish Aid-South Africa Bursary Support Programme

Irish Aid-UNICEF HIV Prevention Projects - Ghana

Kilimanjaro Christian Medical Centre – Tanzania

National Committee for Development Education

NGO Co-Financing Scheme – Brazil, Nigeria, Gambia, Belize, El Salvador, Honduras, Cambodia

Pemba Small Livestock – Tanzania

Rural Footbridges – Lesotho

Refugee Agency

Southern African Subregion Infoterra Network

Tanga Coastal Zone Conservation and Development Programme TB Control Programme – Lesotho

1998 EVALUATIONS

Association of Western European Parliamentarians for Action against Apartheid

Department of Labour Support Programme - South Africa

Development Studies Centre at Kimmage Manor/Training Centre for Development Co-operation (Arusha)

Masters in Policy Studies at Southern African Institute of Policy Studies

Medical Laboratory Supplies

National Community Water and Sanitation Training Institute, Pietersburg – South Africa

NGO Co-financing Scheme – Ethiopia, Lesotho, South Africa, Tanzania, Zambia and Zimbabwe

Rehabilitation Activities in Gedo Region - Somalia

Roads Projects – Ethiopia, Lesotho, Tanzania and Uganda

Sector-Wide Approaches and Financial Accountability

Synthesis Paper - Zimbabwe

Water Sector in Sub-Saharan Africa

ANNEX II

STATISTICS OF AID AND OTHER FLOWS

Table II-1. **Total financial flows**

$ million at current prices and exchanges rates

Net disbursements

Ireland	1981-82	1986-87	1993	1994	1995	1996	1997
Total official flows	**37**	**57**	**90**	**124**	**174**	**180**	**188**
Official development assistance	37	57	81	109	153	179	187
Bilateral	11	26	41	56	88	114	120
Multilateral	26	31	41	53	65	65	67
Official aid	**n.a.**	**n.a.**	**9**	**16**	**21**	**1**	**1**
Bilateral			0	0	2	1	1
Multilateral			8	15	19	-	-
Other official flows	-	-	-	-	-	-	-
Bilateral	-	-	-	-	-	-	-
Multilateral	-	-	-	-	-	-	-
Grants by NGOs	-	**23**	**25**	**52**	**46**	**68**	**56**
Private flows at market terms	-	**16**	**22**	**37**	**48**	**125**	**80**
Bilateral: *of which*	-	16	22	37	48	125	80
Direct investment	-	-	-	-	-	-	-
Export credits	-	16	22	37	48	-	-
Multilateral	-	-	-	-	-	-	-
Total flows	**37**	**96**	**137**	**214**	**268**	**372**	**324**
for reference:							
ODA (at constant 1996 $ million)	*68*	*79*	*91*	*118*	*155*	*179*	*194*
ODA (as a % of GNP)	*0.21*	*0.23*	*0.20*	*0.25*	*0.29*	*0.31*	*0.31*
Total flows (as a % of GNP) (a)	*0.21*	*0.39*	*0.32*	*0.46*	*0.46*	*0.64*	*0.54*

a. To countries eligible for ODA.

ODA net disbursements
at constant 1996 prices and exchange rates and as a share of GNP

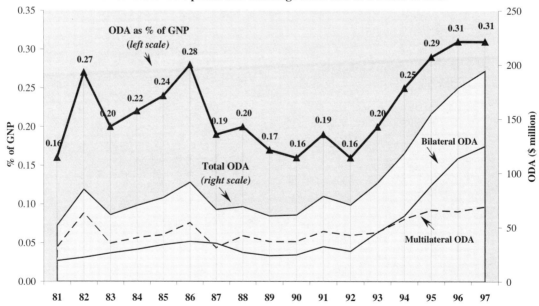

Source: OECD.

Table II-2. **ODA by main categories**

Gross disbursements

Ireland	Constant 1996 $ million					Per cent share					Total DAC 1997%
	1993	1994	1995	1996	1997	1993	1994	1995	1996	1997	
Bilateral	**45**	**61**	**89**	**114**	**125**	**50**	**51**	**57**	**64**	**64**	**71**
Project and programme aid											
Grants	3	3	17	13	20	4	3	11	7	10	13
Loans	-	-	-	-	-	-	-	-	-	-	15
Technical co-operation	25	36	53	67	76	27	31	34	38	39	23
Developmental Food aid (a)	2	1	1	-	-	2	1	1	-	-	2
Emergency and Distress relief (a)	6	9	8	16	12	6	8	5	9	6	4
Action relating to debt	-	-	-	-	2	-	-	-	-	1	6
Core support to NGOs	4	1	1	0	0	4	1	0	0	0	2
Administrative costs	4	5	6	14	12	4	4	4	8	6	5
Other grants	3	5	3	3	3	3	4	2	2	2	2
Multilateral	**46**	**58**	**66**	**65**	**69**	**50**	**49**	**43**	**36**	**36**	**29**
UN agencies	7	10	15	15	18	8	9	10	8	9	7
EC	29	41	44	41	41	32	34	29	23	21	9
World Bank group	9	7	7	7	8	10	6	4	4	4	8
Regional development banks (b)	-	-	-	-	-	-	-	-	-	-	3
Other multilateral	-	-	-	2	3	-	-	-	1	2	2
Total gross ODA	**91**	**118**	**155**	**179**	**194**	**100**	**100**	**100**	**100**	**100**	**100**
Repayments	-	-	-	-							
Total net ODA	**91**	**118**	**155**	**179**	**194**						
For reference:											
Aid channelled through NGOs	-	-	-	-	-						
Associated financing (c)	-	-	-	-	-						

a. Emergency food aid included with Developmental Food Aid up to end 1995.
b Excluding EBRD.
c. ODA grants and loans in associated financing packages.

UN Agencies
(1996-97 Average)

UNRWA 4%
UNDP 17%
UNFPA 3%
UNHCR 12%
UNICEF 11%
WFP 10%
Other UN 43%

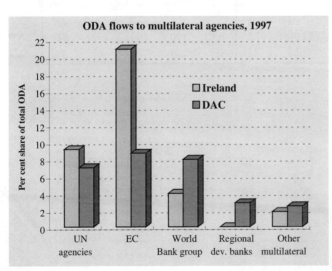

ODA flows to multilateral agencies, 1997

Per cent share of total ODA

☐ Ireland
☐ DAC

UN agencies | EC | World Bank group | Regional dev. banks | Other multilateral

Source: OECD.

Table II-3. Bilateral ODA allocable by region and income groups

Ireland	Constant 1996 $ million					Per cent share					Total DAC
	1993	1994	1995	1996	1997	1993	1994	1995	1996	1997	1997%
Africa	30	40	61	75	93	85	87	81	81	86	**38**
Sub-Saharan Africa	30	40	61	75	93	85	87	81	80	86	**30**
North Africa	0	0	0	0	0	0	0	0	0	0	**8**
Asia	2	4	6	6	7	6	8	8	6	6	**35**
South and Central Asia	1	1	3	3	3	3	2	4	3	3	**13**
Far East	1	3	3	3	4	3	6	4	3	3	**23**
America	0	1	2	3	3	1	2	3	3	3	**14**
North and Central America	0	1	2	2	2	1	2	2	2	2	**6**
South America	0	0	1	1	1	0	1	1	1	1	**8**
Middle East	0	0	2	3	2	1	0	2	4	2	**5**
Oceania	0	0	0	0	0	0	0	0	0	0	**5**
Europe	3	1	4	6	3	7	2	5	7	2	**4**
Total bilateral allocable	**35**	**46**	**75**	**93**	**108**	**100**	**100**	**100**	**100**	**100**	**100**
Least developed	28	39	56	67	83	81	84	75	72	77	**26**
Other low-income	3	5	8	15	13	9	10	11	16	12	**28**
Lower middle-income	3	2	7	6	6	10	5	10	6	5	**36**
Upper middle-income	0	0	4	5	6	0	1	5	6	6	**7**
High-income	0	-	-	0	-	0	-	-	0	-	**3**
For reference:											
Total bilateral	*45*	*63*	*89*	*114*	*125*	*100*	*100*	*100*	*100*	*100*	*100*
of which: Unallocated	*10*	*16*	*13*	*20*	*17*	*23*	*26*	*15*	*18*	*14*	*22*

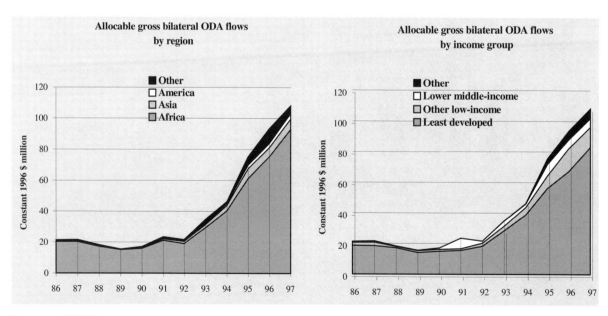

Source: OECD.

Table II-4. Main recipients of bilateral ODA

Gross disbursements, annual averages

Ireland	1986-87				1991-1992				1996-1997		
	Current $ million	Constant 1996 $ mn.	Per cent share		Current $ million	Constant 1996 $ mn.	Per cent share		Current $ million	Constant 1996 $ mn.	Per cent share
Lesotho	4.0	5.5	25.8	Tanzania	4.5	4.7	20.9	Ethiopia	14.8	15.1	15.0
Zambia	3.0	4.2	19.5	Lesotho	3.7	3.9	17.1	Tanzania	11.1	11.3	11.2
Tanzania	2.9	4.0	18.7	Zambia	3.3	3.5	15.4	Zambia	10.3	10.5	10.4
Sudan	2.2	3.1	14.2	Egypt	2.5	2.7	11.3	Lesotho	7.6	7.8	7.7
Zimbabwe	0.9	1.2	5.6	Sudan	1.3	1.4	6.1	Uganda	7.4	7.5	7.4
Top 5 recipients	**13**	**18**	**84**	**Top 5 recipients**	**15**	**16**	**71**	**Top 5 recipients**	**51**	**52**	**52**
Kenya	0.3	0.4	2.0	Ethiopia	0.9	0.9	4.1	Rwanda	4.7	4.8	4.8
Rwanda	0.2	0.3	1.4	Somalia	0.7	0.7	3.3	South Africa	4.5	4.6	4.6
Burundi	0.2	0.3	1.3	Zimbabwe	0.5	0.5	2.3	Mozambique	4.4	4.6	4.5
Ethiopia	0.2	0.3	1.3	Kenya	0.5	0.5	2.2	Bosnia-Herzegovina	4.1	4.1	4.1
Bangladesh	0.1	0.2	0.9	Cambodia	0.5	0.5	2.1	Zimbabwe	2.4	2.4	2.4
Top 10 recipients	**14**	**20**	**91**	**Top 10 recipients**	**18**	**19**	**85**	**Top 10 recipients**	**71**	**73**	**72**
Gambia	0.1	0.2	0.8	Bangladesh	0.3	0.4	1.5	Kenya	2.3	2.3	2.3
Peru	0.1	0.2	0.7	Iran	0.3	0.4	1.5	Palestinian Adm. Areas	2.1	2.1	2.1
Sierra Leone	0.1	0.2	0.7	Sts Ex-Yugoslavia	0.3	0.3	1.4	Sudan	2.0	2.0	2.0
China	0.1	0.1	0.6	Uganda	0.2	0.2	1.0	Nigeria	1.7	1.7	1.7
Ghana	0.1	0.1	0.6	Turkey	0.2	0.2	0.7	Burundi	1.6	1.6	1.6
Top 15 recipients	**15**	**20**	**94**	**Top 15 recipients**	**20**	**21**	**91**	**Top 15 recipients**	**81**	**82**	**82**
Uganda	0.1	0.1	0.6	Nigeria	0.2	0.2	0.7	Cambodia	1.5	1.5	1.5
Botswana	0.1	0.1	0.5	Mozambique	0.1	0.2	0.7	Angola	1.1	1.2	1.1
India	0.1	0.1	0.5	Malawi	0.1	0.2	0.5	Bangladesh	1.0	1.1	1.1
Liberia	0.1	0.1	0.4	Namibia	0.1	0.1	0.5	Congo, Dem. Rep.	0.9	0.9	0.9
Nigeria	0.1	0.1	0.4	India	0.1	0.1	0.5	Brazil	0.8	0.9	0.8
Top 20 recipients	**15**	**21**	**97**	**Top 20 recipients**	**20**	**21**	**94**	**Top 20 recipients**	**86**	**88**	**87**
Total (50 recipients)	**16**	**21**	**100**	**Total (63 recipients)**	**22**	**23**	**100**	**Total (105 recipients)**	**99**	**101**	**100**
Unallocated	11	15		Unallocated	7	8		Unallocated	18	19	
Total bilateral gross	**26**	**36**		**Total bilateral gross**	**29**	**30**		**Total bilateral gross**	**117**	**119**	

Source: OECD.

Table II-5. **Bilateral ODA by major purposes**
at current prices and exchange rates

Disbursements, annual averages

Ireland	1986-87		1991-92		1996		
	$ million	Per cent	$ million	Per cent	$ million	Per cent	Total DAC per cent
Social infrastructure & services	**11**	**43**	**12**	**44**	**54**	**53**	**32**
Education	5	22	7	26	20	20	12
of which: basic education	-	-	-	-	-	-	1
Health	2	8	2	8	16	16	5
of which: basic health	-	-	-	-	-	-	2
Population programmes	-	-	0	0	0	0	1
Water supply & sanitation	1	3	1	4	7	7	7
Government & civil society	1	4	1	3	2	2	3
Other social infrastructure & services	1	6	1	4	8	8	4
Economic infrastructure & services	**0**	**1**	**2**	**6**	**8**	**8**	**25**
Transport & storage	0	0	1	4	5	5	13
Communications	0	0	0	0	0	0	2
Energy	-	-	0	1	1	1	8
Banking & financial services	-	-	-	-	2	2	1
Business & other services	0	0	0	1	-	-	1
Production sectors	**6**	**24**	**3**	**11**	**7**	**7**	**14**
Agriculture, forestry & fishing	5	19	2	7	6	6	10
Industry, mining & construction	1	3	1	3	1	1	2
Trade & tourism	1	2	0	1	0	0	2
Other	-	-	0	0	-	-	0
Multisector	**-**	**-**	**2**	**9**	**3**	**3**	**6**
Commodity and programme aid	**-**	**-**	**3**	**11**	**-**	**-**	**5**
Action relating to debt	**-**	**-**	**-**	**-**	**-**	**-**	**6**
Emergency assistance	**1**	**4**	**2**	**9**	**16**	**16**	**5**
Administrative costs of donors	**3**	**13**	**2**	**8**	**14**	**13**	**5**
Support to NGOs	**3**	**14**	**1**	**2**	**0**	**0**	**1**
Total bilateral allocable	**24**	**100**	**28**	**100**	**102**	**100**	**100**
For reference:							
Total bilateral	*26*	*46*	*28*	*40*	*114*	*64*	*79*
of which: Unallocated	*2*	*3*	*1*	*1*	*12*	*6*	*7*
Total multilateral	*31*	*54*	*43*	*60*	*65*	*36*	*21*
Total ODA	*57*	*100*	*71*	*100*	*179*	*100*	*100*

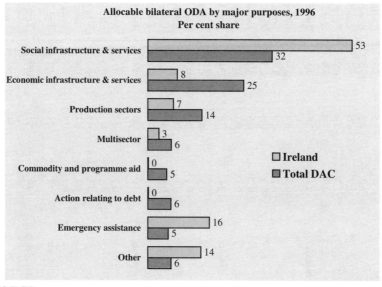

Allocable bilateral ODA by major purposes, 1996
Per cent share

- Social infrastructure & services — 53 / 32
- Economic infrastructure & services — 8 / 25
- Production sectors — 7 / 14
- Multisector — 3 / 6
- Commodity and programme aid — 0 / 5
- Action relating to debt — 0 / 6
- Emergency assistance — 16 / 5
- Other — 14 / 6

□ Ireland ▪ Total DAC

Source: OECD.

Table II-6. Comparative aid performance

| | Official development assistance | | | Grant element of ODA (commitments) 1996 | Share of multilateral aid 1997 | | | | ODA to LLDCs Bilateral and through multilateral agencies 1997 | | Net disbursements Official aid 1997 | |
| | 1997 | | 91-92 to 96-97 Ave. annual % change in real terms | | % of ODA | | % of GNP | | | | | |
	$ million	% of GNP		% (a)	(b)	(c)	(b)	(c)	% of ODA	% of GNP	$ million	% of GNP
Australia	1 061	0.28	-1.2	100.0	26.9		0.08		18.8	0.05	0	0.00
Austria	527	0.26	-2.8	96.6	41.9	23.5	0.11	0.06	17.4	0.04	181	0.09
Belgium	764	0.31	-2.7	98.6	42.7	17.6	0.13	0.05	26.8	0.08	59	0.02
Canada	2 045	0.34	-4.0	100.0	40.6		0.14		22.9	0.08	157	0.03
Denmark	1 637	0.97	3.7	100.0	38.3	32.9	0.37	0.32	29.7	0.29	133	0.08
Finland	379	0.33	-11.9	100.0	47.2	34.5	0.15	0.11	24.4	0.08	71	0.06
France	6 307	0.45	-4.2	87.7	24.3	10.3	0.11	0.05	22.0	0.10	574	0.04
Germany	5 857	0.28	-3.9	88.9	37.9	15.2	0.11	0.04	19.4	0.05	660	0.03
Ireland	187	0.31	20.1	100.0	35.6	14.8	0.11	0.05	47.8	0.15	1	0.00
Italy	1 266	0.11	-12.3	98.2	64.1	15.7	0.07	0.02	25.6	0.03	241	0.02
Japan	9 358	0.22	-5.8	78.4	30.0		0.07		18.9	0.04	84	0.00
Luxembourg	95	0.55	15.0	100.0	30.0	14.8	0.16	0.08	29.2	0.16	2	0.01
Netherlands	2 947	0.81	1.4	100.0	27.6	18.9	0.22	0.15	26.9	0.22	7	0.00
New Zealand	154	0.26	0.9	100.0	26.6		0.07		22.8	0.06	0	0.00
Norway	1 306	0.86	0.5	99.2	29.9		0.26		39.4	0.34	55	0.04
Portugal	250	0.25	-2.6	100.0	34.9	10.4	0.09	0.03	66.1	0.16	18	0.02
Spain	1 234	0.24	-0.7	64.9	38.0	12.0	0.09	0.03	16.3	0.04	3	0.00
Sweden	1 731	0.79	-2.5	100.0	30.2	24.8	0.24	0.20	29.7	0.23	148	0.07
Switzerland	911	0.34	-3.1	100.0	36.8		0.13		32.6	0.11	75	0.03
United Kingdom	3 433	0.26	-0.3	100.0	42.4	21.4	0.11	0.06	22.5	0.06	337	0.03
United States	6 878	0.09	-8.9	99.6	28.2		0.02		19.5	0.02	2 516	0.03
Total DAC	48 324	0.22	-4.6	89.7	33.1	23.2	0.07	0.05	22.6	0.05	5 322	0.02
Memo: Average country effort		0.40										

Notes:
a. Excluding debt reorganisation.
b. Including European Community.
c. Excluding European Community.

Source: OECD.

Figure II-1. **Net ODA from DAC countries in 1997**

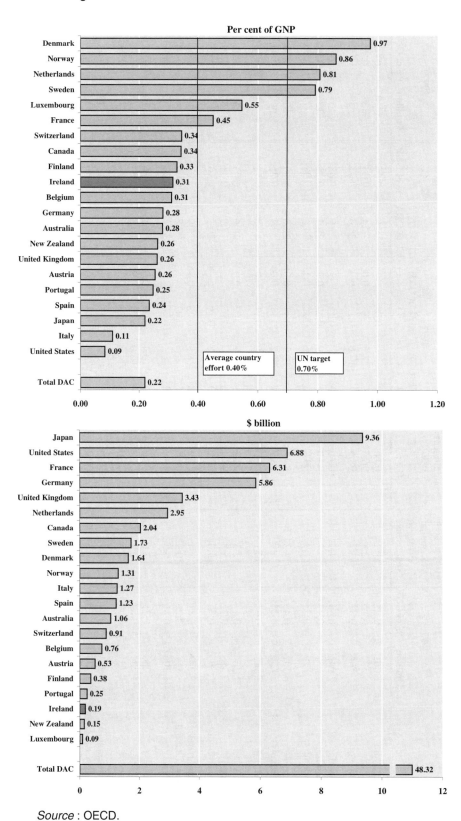

Source : OECD.

PRESS RELEASE OF THE DAC PEER REVIEW OF IRELAND

This year, Ireland marks the 25th anniversary of its official aid programme. Over the last five years, the volume of Ireland's official development assistance (ODA) has risen by an average of 20 per cent a year in real terms, the most rapid growth by a Member of the OECD's Development Assistance Committee (DAC). Preliminary data indicate that Ireland's development co-operation reached 0.30 per cent of GNP in 1998, nearly double its 1992 level, and is projected to reach 0.35 per cent in 1999.

After six years of impressive growth in volume and improvement in quality, most of the increase in aid in 1999 is being used for debt relief measures, European Union contributions, emergency humanitarian assistance, and support for refugees in Ireland, rather than for allocations for the long-term development programmes administered by the Department of Foreign Affairs.

A review of Ireland's development co-operation policies and programme was held on 21 June by the DAC. The Chairman of the DAC, Mr. Jean-Claude Faure, summarised the Committee's findings:

- Irish Aid sets high standards for its official aid programme and is endeavouring to put the partnership approach into practice in its area-based programmes and through its support for sector-wide approaches. Its rising budget is a reflection of Ireland's commitment to reducing poverty in developing countries, and the potential for further growth is supported by Ireland's strong economic performance, coupled with solid political and public support.

- The concern for quality and results in Irish Aid also strengthens the base for further growth. Consistent with the DAC strategy -- *Shaping the 21st Century: The Contribution of Development Co-operation* -- the programme focuses on poverty reduction and is oriented towards the social sectors and human rights and democratisation. Gender equality and environmental sustainability are recognised at the policy level and are reflected in programmes.

- Ireland has worked out good systems for promoting coherence in its policies which impact on developing countries, as well as among its various channels for delivering aid. The Committee encouraged Ireland to pursue its leadership in this area.

- Two main challenges now confront the Irish Aid programme: how best to grow, and how best to manage that growth.

Drawing on the experience of other DAC Members, the Committee discussed the options open to Ireland and recommended that:

- A written implementation programme, up-dating *Irish Aid: Consolidation and Growth* of 1993, and a government-wide commitment to promote development and reduce poverty as priority goals would give clear direction for future growth in the aid programme.

- Irish Aid should maintain and enhance its focused nature. Even a modest increase in the number of priority countries should be evaluated carefully. In its priority countries, Irish Aid has the potential to play a more significant role in co-ordination activities at the national level to share with other donors the benefit of its experience.

- To maintain and secure the better quality and volume of Irish aid in the 1990s, the Irish authorities now need to give high priority to strengthening staffing levels, skill mixes, career prospects and organisational structures for the programme.

- Ireland pursue its consideration of joining the African Development Bank.

- Irish Aid promote a deeper culture of evaluation, monitoring of results and incorporating lessons learnt, together with partners -- including in area-based programmes where Irish Aid specialises.

Ireland's Delegation for the Review was led by Ms. Margaret Hennessy, Assistant Secretary, Development Co-operation Division, Department of Foreign Affairs. The examining countries were Finland and Spain.

DESCRIPTION OF KEY TERMS

The following brief descriptions of the main development co-operation terms used in this publication are provided for general background information. Full definitions of these and other related terms can be found in the "Glossary of Key Terms and Concepts" published in the DAC's annual Development Co-operation Report.

ASSOCIATED FINANCING: The combination of OFFICIAL DEVELOPMENT ASSISTANCE, whether GRANTS or LOANS, with any other funding to form finance packages.

DAC (DEVELOPMENT ASSISTANCE COMMITTEE): The committee of the OECD which deals with development co-operation matters. A description of its aims and a list of its Members are given at the front of this volume.

DAC LIST OF AID RECIPIENTS: A two-part List of Aid Recipients was introduced by the DAC with effect from 1 January 1994. Part I of the List is presented in the following categories (the word "countries" includes territories):

> **LLDCs:** Least Developed Countries. Group established by the United Nations. To be classified as an LLDC, countries must fall below thresholds established for income, economic diversification and social development.

> **Other LICs:** Other Low-Income Countries. Includes all non-LLDC countries with per capita GNP less than USD 765 in 1995 (World Bank Atlas basis).

> **LMICs:** Lower Middle-Income Countries, i.e. with GNP per capita (World Bank Atlas basis) between USD 766 and USD 3 035 in 1995.

> **UMICs:** Upper Middle-Income Countries, i.e. with GNP per capita (World Bank Atlas basis) between USD 3 036 and USD 9 385 in 1995.

> **HICs:** High-Income Countries, i.e. with GNP per capita (World Bank Atlas basis) more than USD 9 385 in 1995.

Part II of the List comprises "Countries in Transition". These comprise: i) more advanced Central and Eastern European Countries and the New Independent States of the former Soviet Union; and ii) more advanced developing countries.

DEBT REORGANISATION: Any action officially agreed between creditor and debtor that alters the terms previously established for repayment. This may include forgiveness, rescheduling or refinancing.

DISBURSEMENT: The release of funds to, or the purchase of goods or services for a recipient; by extension, the amount thus spent. They may be recorded **gross** (the total amount disbursed over a given accounting period) or **net** (less any repayments of LOAN principal during the same period).

EXPORT CREDITS: LOANS for the purpose of trade and which are not represented by a negotiable financial instrument. Frequently these LOANS bear interest at a rate subsidised by the government of the creditor country as a means of promoting exports.

GRANTS: Transfers made in cash, goods or services for which no repayment is required.

GRANT ELEMENT: Reflects the **financial terms** of a commitment: interest rate, maturity and grace period (i.e. the interval to the first repayment of principal). The grant element is nil for a LOAN carrying an interest rate of 10 per cent; it is 100 per cent for a GRANT; and it lies between these two limits for a LOAN at less than 10 per cent interest.

LOANS: Transfers for which repayment is required. Data on **net loans** include deductions for repayments of principal (but not payment of interest) on earlier loans.

OFFICIAL AID: Flows which meet the conditions of eligibility for inclusion in OFFICIAL DEVELOPMENT ASSISTANCE, except that the recipients are on Part II of the DAC LIST OF AID RECIPIENTS.

OFFICIAL DEVELOPMENT ASSISTANCE (ODA): GRANTS or LOANS to countries and territories on Part I of the DAC LIST OF AID RECIPIENTS (developing countries) provided by the official sector with the promotion of economic development and welfare as the main objective and which are at concessional financial terms (if a LOAN, having a GRANT ELEMENT of at least 25 per cent).

OTHER OFFICIAL FLOWS (OOF): Transactions by the official sector with countries on the DAC LIST OF AID RECIPIENTS which do not meet the conditions for eligibility as OFFICIAL DEVELOPMENT ASSISTANCE or OFFICIAL AID.

PARTIALLY UNTIED AID: OFFICIAL DEVELOPMENT ASSISTANCE (or OFFICIAL AID) for which the associated goods and services must be procured in the donor country or among a restricted group of other countries, which must however include substantially all recipient countries.

PRIVATE FLOWS: Consist of the following flows at market terms financed out of private sector resources:

> **Direct investment:** Investment made to acquire or add to a lasting interest in an enterprise in a country on the DAC LIST OF AID RECIPIENTS.

> **Bilateral portfolio investment:** Includes bank lending, and the purchase of shares, bonds and real estate.

> **Multilateral portfolio investment:** This covers the transactions of the private non-bank and bank sector in the securities issued by multilateral institutions.

> **Private export credits:** See EXPORT CREDITS.

TECHNICAL CO-OPERATION: Includes both i) GRANTS to nationals of recipient countries receiving education or training at home or abroad, and ii) payments to consultants, advisers and similar personnel as well as teachers and administrators serving in recipient countries.

TIED AID: Official GRANTS or LOANS where procurement of the goods or services involved is limited to the donor country or to a group of countries which does not include substantially all recipient countries.

UNTIED AID: OFFICIAL DEVELOPMENT ASSISTANCE (or OFFICIAL AID) for which the associated goods and services may be fully and freely procured in substantially all countries.

VOLUME: Unless otherwise stated, data are expressed in current United States dollars. Data in national currencies are converted into dollars using annual average exchange rates. To give a truer idea of the volume of flows over time, some data are presented in **constant prices and exchange rates**, with a reference year specified. This means that adjustment has been made to cover both inflation between the year in question and the reference year, and changes in the exchange rate between the currency concerned and the United States dollar over the same period.

OECD PUBLICATIONS, 2, rue André-Pascal, 75775 PARIS CEDEX 16
PRINTED IN FRANCE
(43 1999 08 1 P) ISBN 92-64-17118-5 – No. 50871 1999